C000045522

Icarus Rising

New and Selected Work

Nigel Pearce

chipmunkapublishing
the mental health publisher

All rights reserved, no part of this publication may be reproduced by any means, electronic, mechanical photocopying, documentary, film or in any other format without prior written permission of the publisher.

Published by
Chipmunkapublishing
United Kingdom

http://www.chipmunkapublishing.com

Copyright © 2015 Nigel Pearce

ISBN   978-1-78382-154-9

Chipmunkapublishing gratefully acknowledge the support of Arts Council England.

I preface this new collection with two examinations into aesthetics. Firstly prose-fiction and then secondly the aesthetics of poetry. To begin my brief journey I employ the Nobel Prize for Literature as a point of departure for some of my ideas regarding aesthetics and prose writing.

This first thesis examines Modernist and Postmodernist aesthetics as tools for judging literature generally and prose-fiction particularly. I use Pat Barker (1995) *The Ghost Road* and Philip K. Dick (1968*) Do Androids Dream of Electric Sheep* as examples and offer a Marxist critique of the criteria for the awarding of the Nobel Prize for Literature which is seen as the dominant prize in today's conditions. What I am attempting to do is look for an alternative method of formulation judgements on Literature. The original citation for the Nobel Prize for Literature was:
> ...for the most outstanding work, in the ideal direction.
> (Gupta 2005, p. 210).

However 'ideal' should be translated as 'idealistic'. This suggests metaphysical or Idealist Kantian aesthetics. I contend that contrary to Kantian aesthetics, 'art' does not exist outside of material history, rather it is an artefact of production and consumption in a historically specific and concrete 'mode of production'. It is possible to perceive the Nobel Prize for Literature as being formed and reformed by socio-cultural elements because   Allén (1997) illustrates it had constantly reinvented itself to accommodate shifts of 'taste' This was made explicit in 1964 when Jean-Paul Sartre refused the Prize because he maintained it was:
> ...guided by a capitalist western bloc ideology.
> (Johnson 2005, p. 213.)

I shall rather perceive aesthetics as a reflection of socio-economic forces, though determined by the material base as Engels maintained 'only in the last instant' (Eagleton 1976, pp. 3-6). My readings of Barker (1995) and Dick (1968) allow the necessary logic of my methodology, 'Historical Materialism', to develop because the dialectical contradictions present are yet to be resolved; we are still living in the epoch of class conflict. My methodology is derived from Marx and Engels in *The German Ideology*:
> The production of ideas, of conceptions, of consciousness,
> is at first directly interwoven with the material activity and the
> material intercourse of men ... The same applies to mental production

3

as expressed in the language of politics, laws, morality, religion,
metaphysics, etc. of a people.
(Johnson p, 220.)

Modernism is a multitudinous and fragmented narrative developed and contested in Brecht, (1978) Lukacs (1963) and in the discoveries of Sigmund Freud. I also note postmodernism in Jean-François Lyotard (1979) and his concepts of the collapse of the meta-narrative and the rise of the micro-narrative in the postmodernist era. These ideas will be complexified and challenged by Fredrick Jameson (1991) *Post Modernism or, the Logic of Late Capitalism*. Alex Callinicos (1989) *Against Post Modernism* provides a necessary theoretical corrective to the postmodernist thesis promoting 'the radical Enlightenment', and on this foundation I construct new criteria for the Nobel Prize: "The literary text which most persuasively promotes social transformation" and award the Prize to Philip K. Dick (1968*) Do Androids Dream of Electric Sheep*. This is because it exhibits both the 'cognitive estrangement', a variant on Brechtian 'alienation-effect', reflecting both on imagined and material worlds and on contradictions, for example, the treatment of Rachel and Prim by Deckard. This text illustrates numerous contradictions that generate dialectical opposites. It delineates a dystopia and thereby creates potential for its opposite a utopian society in the reader's consciousness. This aspiration for a new society when encouraged by engagement with the radical Enlightenment is then realizable in History.

What is my critique of the Kantian Aesthetic? Firstly Kant is significant in that he provided the ideology of the bourgeois writer who apparently exists outside of history and creates 'art' as opposed to the production of artefacts. Aesthetics in this view concern defining 'taste'. For Kant there are two elements as (Johnson 2005, p 202) argues: 1) originality and 2) exemplarity I would add both a) ontology and b) an epistemology. The 'ontology' of art is in the art exists not in its being a 'use-value' but as 'recognition as a work of art' as the Sublime and its epistemology is the stimulation or imaging of the art object. So for Kant, we perceive beauty through our sense-experience, and having an experience of the Sublime universalize it in abstraction. This is a form of 'Objective Idealism', it argues consciousness determines being.

Here is a problem for Kant, yes, aesthetic taste includes a subjective judgement but it cannot be universalized in a social formulation which privileges one class or the atomized and alienated individual writer in capitalism. John Keats (1819) *Ode on a Grecian Urn* encapsulates Kant's view in nascent capitalism:
"Beauty is truth, truth beauty"-that is all

4

Nigel Pearce

Ye know on earth, and all ye need to know
(Keats 1988, p, 346).
However the Enlightenment Project also gave birth to 'market capitalism', the bourgeoisie, and its dialectical opposite the proletariat or 'universal class' which would necessarily develop an objective interest in creating a higher and universal aesthetic. My position is that only 'labour' is creative and has the capacity to create art and thus art is a social practice only realizable when the 'means of production' are socialized. Here Trotsky encapsulates this as practice:

Under Socialism, Literature and art will be tuned to a different
key such as disinterested friendship ...Art then will become the
most perfect ethos for progressive building of life in every field.
(Trotsky 1981, p 60.)

This is congruent with Walter Benjamin in his remark on pre-communist aesthetics:

Every document in civilization is a record of barbarism... A
Historical Materialist therefore dissociates himself from it...
(Benjamin 1991, p. 248).
An example of the bourgeois artist in this period is Oscar Wilde in (Gupta & Johnson 2005 p. 8) 'All art is quite useless.' I prefer, like Alex Callinicos (1989) to locate 'a radicalized Enlightenment tradition':

Used reason as an instrument of liberation. Marx did so more
emphatically: theory, when integrated by means of socialist
organization in the struggle for working class self-emancipation ...but
for Freud too, the patient's development of rational understanding...
was an essential feature of his therapy.
(Callinicos 1989, p. 172.)
Callinicos (2002) *Social Theory* argues the Enlightenment tradition is also indebted to Hegel who wrote:

Contradiction is at the root of all movement and life and
it is only in so far as it contains a Contradiction that
anything moves has impulses and activity.
(Callinicos 2002, p 41.)
My criterion is instrumentalist, but with an aesthetic so I disagree with the view of
Leftist writing which Orwell (1936) argued:

... That art and propaganda are the same thing
(Gupta & Johnson, 2005 p. 6.).
For Marxists like Adorno & Horkheimer (1947) *Dialectic of Enlightenment* the spectre of two world wars, the rise of fascism and Stalinism dashed their belief in the Enlightenment Project:

> Only the conscious horror of destruction creates the correct
> relationship with the dead: unity with them because we, like
> them are the victims of the same condition and the same
> disappointed hope.
> (Braninigan 2007, p. 13).

It was necessary to examine the criteria of aesthetics in Kant and in attempting to achieve discussion of the nature of the canon, the Prize and then provide my alternative. In terms of positioning modernist literature it is impossible without an understanding the impact of Eliot (1920) *The Sacred Wood*:

> This historical sense, which is a sense of the timeless
> and of the temporal and of the timeless and of the
> temporal together is what makes a writer traditional. And
> it is at the same time what makes a writer most acutely
> conscious of his place in time, of his own contemporarily.
> (Gupta & Johnson 2005, p 98.)

So Eliot, the disillusionment in the Enlightenment Project and the apparent triumph of capitalism and consumerism during the 'post-war boom' all must be acknowledged and their implosion into "pastiche' for Fredric Jameson (1992) *Post Modernism or, the Logic of Late Capitalism*, I have some sympathy with Jameson's perspective. Jameson must be understood in the light of Ernest Mandel *Late-Capitalism* (1978) who developed a tripartite model of capitalism. Jameson superimposed another Marxian 'cultural' mode derived from the British Marxist Raymond Williams on this model. Here, for Jameson late-capitalism is culturally 'residual' and he argues:

> Not only are Picasso and Joyce no longer ugly, they now
> strike us, on the whole, as rather "realistic," and this is the
> result of a canonisation and academic institutionalisation of
> the modern movement generally that can be dated to the
> late 1950s.
> (Jameson, 1991 p 4.)

> This is, then, the relief of the postmodern… but it has had its
> price: namely, the primary destruction of modernist formal
> value…the status of art… in order to secure the new productivities
> (Jameson, pp. 317-18).

Thus postmodernism has at its centre an apparent contradiction. This dissertation is positioned in Post W.W 11 literature, but has addressed the questions of aesthetics in both modernism and post-modernist narratives. I agree with Callinicos (1989) that there is a necessity for a renewed Marxist poetics:

> Unless we work toward this kind of revolutionary
> change which would allow the realization of this
> potential in a transformed world, there is little left for

us to do, except, like Lyotard and Baudrillard, to fiddle
while Rome burns.
(Callinicos 1989, p. 174.)

I shall examine my runner-up first which is Pat Barker The Ghost Road, would be a worthy winner if the existing criteria of the Nobel Prize stood and is indeed a fine novel. Barker wrote:

I didn't see the point of writing an anti-war novel that only
examined the tragedy that is almost part of the fabric of our
national consciousness.
(Monteith, 2002. p. 27).

Barker, I argue, rejects conventional Realism in favour of micro-narratives as we see from her shift from third-person account to Priors first person account at the beginning of Chapter Seven. We read the naturalistic first person diary entries of Prior as creating a sense of intimacy between him and the reader and commenting on the process of writing:

First-person narrators don't die, so long as we keep telling the story
of our own life we remain safe.
(Barker 1995, p. 115).

These are juxtaposed with feverish memories of Dr. Rivers recounting his anthropological pre-war expedition to Melanesia to research head-hunters who
ironically are 'dying through a lack of war'.

Dr. Rivers ponders:
Was this the suppressed memory?
(Barker, p. 96).

After recalling a minor trauma with his father and then remembering attending church with his father and the iconography in his father's churches:

In one of his father's churches, St Faith's, at Maidstone,
the window to the left of the altar shows Abraham with the
knife raised to slay his son, and, below the human figures,
a ram caught in the thicket by his horns.
(Barker, p. 104).

Abraham here is a metaphor for Dr Rivers and Isaac for Prior but Rivers rather does sacrifice his sons just as on the island of Vao 'bastard sons' are sacrificed (Barker 1995, pp103-4).He cures them of their trauma only to return to France to die and kill.

Then the positioning of a newspaper headline praising the war in quasi-erotic jingoistic language is placed at the beginning of Chapter Fourteen:

SHEER FIGHTING
BOTH SIDES PAY THE PRICE

HUNS WAIT FOR THE BAYONET
(Barker, p. 203).

It is a powerful insertion of text as it is then placed layer upon layer with the realities of war in Priors diaries without any narrartive sequence. Finally, (Barker 1995 p, 276) Njiru the crippled witch-doctor whom Rivers recollected from the anthropological pre-war expedition comes to haunt the ward as Dr. Rivers sits, an emasculated analyst/doctor who has sent his patients back to France to their deaths and cannot anaesthetise the pain of their physical mutilations either:

Grey light tinged with rosy pink seeps in through the tall windows. Rivers, slumped at the night nurses' station, struggles to stay awake.

The edge of sleep he hears Njiru's voice, repeating the words of the exorcism of Ave. O Sumbi! O Gesese! O Palapoko! O Gorepoko! O you Ngengere at the root of the sky. Go down, depart ye. And there, suddenly, not separate from the ward, not in any way ghostly, not in fashion blong tomate, but him in every particular, advancing down the ward of the Empire Hospital...

(Barker, p. 276).

For Barker neither Primitivism nor Modernism has the solution because of the postmodern rejection of the radical Enlightenment tradition of social transformation.

Pat Barker dismisses 'stream of consciousness' techniques of High Modernism. Instead, Barker embraces both a post-colonialist and post-modernist shifting of perspective rooted in both the objective and subjective. She is employing a Panoptic methodology. Mark Rawlinson Pat Barker: New British Fiction argues:

Barker's imagined great War is a revisionist historical construct, which examines versions of the war to reveal a secret war, the dimensions of 1914-18 which have been overlooked by different ressures created by official remembrance, the literature of protest, and an abiding train of popular militarism in Britain.

(Rawlinson 2010, p 68).

Thus, I argue that Pat Barker's literary techniques and orientation are those of a post-modernist, post-colonial novel, which can be located as 'factual fictions' (Johnson 2005 p. 371.), or 'metafiction'. Prescott notes as significant the subtitling by Norman Mailer (1968) Armies of the Night with 'History as a Novel, the Novel as History' (Johnson p. 371). I note an abundance of apparently Freudian references to Dr. Rivers; however the historical Rivers (1923) *Conflict and Dream* rejected Sigmund Freud (1921) *Beyond the Pleasure Principle*. Freud extended his dream methodology to incorporate a psycho-biological conflict:

Nigel Pearce

The goal of all life is death

(Freud 1995, p. 613).

Without a dialectical materialist explanation of the war that Lenin (1916) located in 'moribund' or late capitalism in the export of Capital from monopoly capitalist states and therefore creating imperialist conflict psychoanalysis was to be stretched to explain why humanity had slain millions of young men. Pat Barker really examined a feature of 'monopoly capitalism', world war, from the perspective of the post-modern novel in which she finds no coherent explanatory meta-narrative.

I shall now show why and how Philip K. Dick (1968) *Do Androids Dream of Electric Sheep* fulfills my revised criteria for winning the Nobel Prize for Literature. He developed both an innovative new poetic in synthesizing a form of popular literature, Science Fiction, with philosophical issues such as class, religion and alienation often associated with the radical Enlightenment. He therefore meets my criteria: "The literary text which most persuasively promotes social transformation". Although Dick (1968) is certainly not a piece of 'Socialist Realism' which the Marxist critic George Lukacs (1963) would acquiesce to such as Gorky (1906) *Mother*. It transcends those boundaries to achieve the same consequences using 'cognitive estrangement'. What Science Fiction does is to challenge the hegemony of the cultural domain of late-capitalism. A Marxist definition of Science Fiction was articulated by Darko Suvin (1979):

A literary genre whose necessary and sufficient conditions are the presence of estrangement and cognition.

(Suvin 1979, p 7).

.In other words, Raymond Williams (1980):

It must cause a crisis of possibility, a reworking in imagination, of all forms and conditions.

(Williams 1980, p. 209).

What Science Fiction does then is show us a view of reality after being defamiliarized and then act as a mirror in which we see ourselves and the society we live in and thus I read Dick (1968) in the light of these Marxist commentators.

Hence we are shown by Dick (1968) a world devastated by 'World War Terminus' which was a very real possibility in 1968 with Mutually Assured Destruction (MAD) after an exchange of nuclear weapons between the U.S.A and U.S.S.R.

Plekhanov commented:

The social mentality of an age is conditioned by its social conditions, this is nowhere quite as evident as in the history of art and literature.

(Eagleton 1976, p. 6).

9

In the wake of the war human colonization of other planets is necessary because of the nuclear fallout. Humans are given the choice:

Emigrate or degenerate! The choice is yours.

(Dick. 1968, p. 6).

The world has been devastated by an imperialist war, the 'highest stage of capitalism' explained in Lenin (1916) *Imperialism, the Highest Stage of Capitalism* and social polarization is complete. This is manifested by dialectical 'doubles'. Rick Deckard and John R. Isidore, both humans but Rick is of the privelleged 'labour aristocracy' while Isoidre is a 'special'. The latter are 'damaged' as a result of being damaged by nuclear fallout, but are a metaphor for the proletariat and lumpen-proletariat in late-capitalism. Supraexploited and demonized. Isidore does manual work:

Classed as biologically unacceptable.... Once pegged

a special, a citizen, even if accepting sterilization,

dropped out of history. He ceased, in effect, to be a

member of mankind.

(Dick 1968, p. 14).

Rick is described by his wife as:

a crude cop... You're worse, his wife

said.....You're a

murderer hired by the cops.

I have never killed a human in my life....

Iran said, 'Just those poor Andy's'.

(Dick, p.1).

Androids ('Andy's') are built by the Rosen Association which is the incarnation of 'accumulation for accumulation's sake' (Marx, Capital, Ch., 32) as servants on Mars to the colonisers, another 'dialectical' double, Nexus-6 androids look like humans, are highly intelligent desiring freedom from slavery imposed by their creators.

There's a double here as well Rachel, who is an Android member of the Rosen Association who sleeps with Rick and Prim who he 'retires':

'An android doesn't care what happens to another android,

hat's one of the indications we look for.

(Dick, p 99).

Rick says this as he questions Luba Luft, an opera singer he admires but 'retires'. Rick ultimately questions the dominant ideology:

Do androids dream? Rick asked himself

(Dick, p. 183).

The Situationalist Debord (1992) *The Society of The Spectacle* argued that Marx's theory of alienation had to now encompass the:

Pseudo-needs imposed by modern consumerism...an

unlimited artificiality which overpowers any living desire.
(Debord 1992, p. 34).

Deckard's 'electric sheep' is significant here as is the 'mood organ' which humans use to generate emotions at will. We are 'shown' the contradictions of late-capitalism by defamiliarization and respond dialectically.

I delineated criteria for the Nobel Prize, understood it related to Kantian aesthetics, constructed a Marxist critique, extended this to Postmodernism, made a reading of Barker (1995) which saw it as potentially fulfilling the original criteria given 'shifts in taste' and seen her novel as postmodernist. Then appraised the developments in Marxist theory regarding Science Fiction as a genre, 'read' Dick (1968) in this light and therefore as his novel inspires the reader to contemplate a potentiality for social transformation in the radical Enlightenment tradition awarded him the Prize because Marx argues cogently (1852):

> The social revolution... cannot take its poetry
> from the past but only from the future.
> Marx (2007) p 331.

Icarus Rising

Bibliography.

Allén, S Topping Shakespeare? Aspects of the Nobel Prize for Literature".*Nobelprize.org.*

Barker, P (1995) *The Ghost Road,* London: Penguin.

Benjamin, W (1999) *Illuminations*, London: Vintage Books.

Bould, M & Mieville, C (eds) (2009) *Red Planets: Marxism and Science Fiction*, London: Plato Books.

Braninigan (2007) Pat Barker's Regeneration Trilogy in Lane, R. J, Mengham and P, Tew (eds) *Contemporary British Fiction*, Cambridge: Polity Press.

Brecht, B (1978*) Brecht on Theatre: The development of An Aesthetic*, ed. and trans. by J.Willett, London: Methuen.

Callinicos, A (1989) *Against Postmodernism: A Marxist Critique*, Cambridge: Polity Press.

Callinicos, A (2002) *Social Theory: A Historical introduction*, Cambridge: Polity Press.

Debord, G ([1967]1992) *The Society of The Spectacle*, trans. Ken Knob, London: Rebel Press.

Dick, P, K ([1968] 2001) *Do Androids Dream of Electric Sheep?* S.F. Masterworks, London: Gallanez/Orion.
Eagleton, T (1976) *Marxism and Literary Criticism*, London: Routledge.
Elliot, T.S [1920] 1960) *The Sacred Wood,* London: Methuen.

Freud, S (1995) *The Freud Reader*, London: Vintage Originals.

Gorky, M ([1906]1983) *Mother*, Moscow: Raduga Publishers.

Gupta, S & Johnson, D (2005) A *Twentieth-century Reader; texts and debates,* Milton Keynes: The Open University.

Jameson, F (1991) *PostmodernisTm or, The Culture of Late Capitalism*, London: Verso.

Johnson, D (2005) *The Popular and the Canonical; debating twentieth century literature, 1940-2000,* Milton Keynes: The Open University.

Keats, J (1988*) The Complete Poems*, London: Penguin Classics

Lenin, V. I (1916) *Imperialism, the Highest Stage of Capitalism*

Lukacs, G (1963) *The Meaning of Contemporary Realism*, trans. John and Necke Mander, London: Merlin

Lyotard, J-F ([1979]1984) *The Postmodern Condition: A Report on Knowledge*, trans. by G. Bennington and B. Massumi, Manchester: Manchester University Press.

Mandel, E (1978) *Late-Capitalism*, London: Verso.

Marx, K ([1843] 1977) A Contribution to Hegel's Critique of Right in Colletti (ed) *Marx Early Writings*, London: Pelican Marx Library.

Marx, K ([1867]1977) *Capital* Volume*1*, London: Pelican Marx Library

Marx, K ([1853]2007) *Selected Works*, Oxford: Oxford University Press.

Monteith, S (2002) *Pat Barker: Writers and their Work*, Plymouth: Northcote House Ltd.

Rawlinson, M (2010) *Pat Barker: New British Fiction*, Basingstoke, Hampshire: Palgrave McMillian.

Suvin, D (1979) *Metamorphosis of Science Fiction: on the Poetics and History of a Literary Genre*, New Haven: Yale University Press.

Trotsky, L (1981*) On Literature and Art*, New York: Pathfinder Press.

Williams, R (1980), 'Utopia and Science Fiction' *in Problems in Materialism and Culture*, London: New Left Books.

Icarus Rising

A second essay will briefly delineate my perspective on poetry and aesthetics. I use the example of Allen Ginsberg's 'Howl' to make my position clear in the context of the Western literary canon. Just what is poetry for?

On the poetics of Allen Ginsberg.

I argue Ginsberg's *Howl* was not a popular 'over-simplification' of poetry regarded by the Canon as high literature. Rather, *Howl* formed a new genre which mirrored other seminal moments in literature connected to different 'modes of production' which had similar ramifications. It significantly altered the American cultural construct, I contend that an aesthetic informed by Trotsky's cultural writing would suggest a Social rather than a cultural revolution is necessary to emancipate literature. I do this in the context of contending perspectives of popular and high culture.

Howl can be understood with Marxist methodology as Caudwell (1937) *Illusion and Reality* associated William Shakespeare with nascent capitalism, 'bourgeois' revolutions permeate the ideas of Wordsworth (1802) *Preface to Lyrical Ballads* and the shocks of Darwinism, Freud and imperialist war informed Modernist literature, particularly avant-garde poetry like T.S.Eliot (1922) *The Waste Land*. The problem of the writer in late-capitalism Trotsky (1981) *Art and Politics* argued was that:

> The decline of bourgeois society means an intolerable exacerbation of social contradictions, which are transformed inevitably into personal contradictions, art suffers most from the decline and decay of bourgeois society. Art cannot save itself...But precisely in this path history has set a formidable snare for the artist.
>
> Trotsky (1981). p 105.

Ginsberg's reply is *Howl*; it resonates within the conversation of literature, *King Lear* (1603):

> Howl, howl, howl! O, you are men of stones;
> Had I your tongues and eyes, I'd use them so
> That heaven's vault should crack.
> Shakespeare (1603) (5.3.2.58-64).

Howl
For
Carl Solomon
1

I saw the best minds of my generation destroyed by madness, starving hysterical naked,

dragging themselves through the Negro streets at
dawn looking for an angry fix, angleheaded hipsters
burning for the ancient heavenly
  connection to the starry dynamo in the machine-
  ery of night

Ginsberg (1956) p. 9

It is the howl of a post-WW 11 avant-garde and employs the poetic
devices of literary tradition but it is refashioned. A 'close reading'
gives us several insights here. They are 'howls' of emotion, of
intense emotion which resonate with William Wordsworth
(1802) *Preface to Lyrical Ballads*:

Poetry is the spontaneous overflow of powerful feelings: it
takes its origin from emotion recollected in tranquility.

William Wordsworth (1980) pp. 410-424.

In Shakespeare (1603) we have a reference to the howling of a man
driven to madness seeking justice from 'heaven's vaults'. Ginsberg
also seeks refuge in chants to the 'Holy' in *Footnote to Howl*. The
thematic howl of a literate madness, seeking divine justice, but not
locating it in a corrupted 'world' runs counterintuitive against the
whole Enlightenment project. Surely Reason and empiricist science
will hear the poet's words. For Americans like Ginsberg the world
could not be explained in these neat confines and as a poet who had
read widely he certainly could not accept the text by text alone
reductionism of the New Criticism after Hiroshima and McCarthyism,
Auschwitz and Stalinism. But what differentiated Ginsberg from other
'Beat' writers in particular Kerouac was that he rejected Kerouac
insistence on 'first thought, best thought'. Ginsberg was influenced
by both Kerouac in terms of first impulse, but also poets like Eliot,
indeed *Howl'* is an attempt at reproducing something of the literary
magnitude of Eliot (1922) *The Waste Land*. I shall therefore argue
against the perspective taken by advocates of Mass Culture Thesis
such as Dwight Macdonald, who argues in (1953) *A Theory of Mass
Culture* and again (1962) *Against the American Grain* that the
collective taste of the 'masses' was reflected in the degraded mass
culture that they consumed and that, therefore, they had no 'interest'
in 'High Culture'. Dwight Macdonald combined an ex-Trotskyist
stance with cultural conservatism and elitism. Also, I argue against a
rightist conservative position which is derived from Matthew Arnold
(1869) *Culture and Anarchy* that has an inherent fear of the popular
and thought civilization needed a secular religion to protect it from
the masses.

'the best that has been thought and said in the
world.'

Arnold (1869) p 6.

It is no accident that Arnold began his *opus magnum* in 1867 after a
period of popular discontent over suffrage rights. Ginsberg's reply

here is the 20th century equivalent to an articulate class response to Arnold:

> who dreamt and made incarnate gaps in Time & Space
>> through images juxtaposed, and trapped the
>> archangel of the soul between 2 visual images
>> and joined the elemental verbs and set the noun
>> and dash of consciousness together jumping
>> with sensation of Pater Omnipotens Aeterna
>> Deus to recreate the syntax and measure of poor
>> human prose...

Ginsberg 1956 p 20.

Arnold and his Leavisite descendants would possibly lost for words, their *Weltanschauung* challenged. Also we can perceive Ginsberg's specialist use of 'strophes' which he defines in Asbee (2005) p.90 as 'a one speech breath thought' which was akin to the jazz improvisation of Miles Davis or Charlie Parker, the black man's 'beat'.

'Form' with regard to these socio-cultural factors was engaged by the New Historicism of Raymond Williams in his 1958 *Forward to Culture and Society*:

> We live in an expanding culture, yet we spend much of
> our energyregretting the fact, rather than seeking to
> understand its nature and conditions.

Lodge (1972) p. 580.

However, my position is not simply that Mass Culture Thesis and the New Criticism were erroneous, but they failed to understand the nuanced nature of 'proletarian literature' which as Trotsky illustrates is complexified:

> Having broken up human relations into atoms, bourgeois
> society,had a great aim for itself. Personal emancipation was
> its name. In reality, all modern literature has been nothing but
> an enlargement of this theme.

Trotsky (1981) pp. 61-62.

My position is that only the proletariat has the creative potential and socially universal nature which allowed Marx to say 'communism has solved the riddle of history' can transcend the limitations of the bourgeois intelligentsia when the social and economic conditions are ripe, that is, in a Socialist society because as Marx argued they are the 'universal class'. For the first time in history was there a social collectivity in whose interest it was to dismantle class society, because 'class' fetters on the workers of the world are their 'chains and it is in their interest 'collectively' to break those chains freeing the whole of society.

Some Marxists misunderstood the nature of the relationship between the popular and the high cultures. Adorno and Horkheimer in

Icarus Rising

Dialectic of Enlightenment saw an implied analogy between Marx's concept of his fetishized 'exchange value' as a commodity and 'use-value' a 'material object'. Then they extrapolated this analogy to the relationship between popular and high culture to the detriment of the popular. Walter Benjamin is better here, seeing the potential for mechanized reproduction to free the poet from the 'aura' from his or her primitivism and allow an engaged mass readership. Also, I will draw a parallel with Maxim Gorky, *Lower Depths* (see Raskin 2004, p.82) and Ginsberg *Howl*, thus Trotsky:

> At the beginning, Gorky was imbued with the romantic
> individualism of the tramp. Nevertheless, he fed the
> early spring revolutionism of the proletariat on the eve of
> 1905, because he helped to awaken individuality in that
> class in which individuality, once awakened,
> seeks contact with other awakened individualities'
>
> Trotsky (1981) p 58-59

For Trotsky the solution to the dichotomy of oversimplification and complexity in literature is resolved in the synthesis of revolution. Ginsberg, unlike Gorky would not be involved in a social revolution (as he may have wished) but a cultural revolution, a revolution of superstructure rather that of social base which left American capitalism weakened but intact. Louis Althusser (2006) *Lenin on Philosophy and Other Essays* commenting on the novels of Solzhenitsyn in (Althusser pp.153-153, 2006) makes the point of the difference between art and knowledge. Literature like Solzhenitsyn's, he argues, may have helped the reader 'feel', 'perceive' the 'cult of personality' in the Soviet Union but doesn't provide the scientific knowledge to understand it. Althusser said art:

> In the language of Spinoza it puts the
> conclusions before the premises.
>
> Althusser (2006) p 153.

Ginsberg achieves this by employing and developing poetic devices, Walt Whitman's 'long-line' which is a non-metrical line of poetry of length which usually employs enjambment, anaphora which is a 'figure of repetition' in which the same word is repeated as in Part 1 'Who' usually at the beginning successive 'lines, clauses or sentences', cauda or the tail-rhyme stanza and a surrealist juxtaposition of images such as 'helium jukebox' (1956).Also Ginsberg aspired to create:

> 'Certain combinations of words and rhythms actually
> have an electrochemical reaction on the body, which
> could catalyze specific states of consciousness.
>
> Ginsberg (2001) p. 31

Brain Jackson (2010) argues: 'the most compelling example of reading "Howl" specially out loud – is the sense of time shifting from the prosaic to the mythical. Lines such as

> who walked all night with their shoes full of blood on
> the snowdeck docks waiting for a door in the
> East River to open to a room full of steamheat
> opium,
>
> Ginsberg (1956) p. 15

He continues 'the rhythmic and trouping artifice of Howl constitute...a suspension of time in which the natural laws occur'. Jackson (2010) pp 312-313). I would add that this is congruent with Ginsberg 'an angry fix' p. 9. Here the assonance and metre suggest the addict's "rush" after their injection.

Therefore I maintain that Ginsberg poetry contradicted the ideas of thinkers such as Mathew Arnold, T. S. Eliot, and William Empson's *Seven Types of Ambiguity* on the Right and renegade ex-Trotskyists like Dwight MacDonald and neo-Marxists Adorno and Horkheimer. I suggest that the neo-Marxism of Louis Althusser enhanced my general understanding of the positioning of the debates regarding the poetry of Ginsberg, particularly *Howl* and that in this context it is possible to comprehend him in a lineage of literati. Finally I argue that Ginsberg created not a simplified poetry for mass consumption and 'narcotization' of literary consciousness, but formed the matrix for a new genre of second wave of 20th century avant-garde writers who took and added to the High Modernism of 1910-39 and created a wedge into the monotonous conformity of 1950's poetry, even poets like Sylvia Plath and Anne Sexton writing confessional verse which were challenging some convention in terms of gender and 'content' i.e. mental illness Plath ([1963] 2004) *Ariel* and Sexton's (1960) *'To Bedlam and part way back',* but were 'straight' rather than 'queer' confessional verse and this is significant for although Ginsberg was unable to create a social revolution he did shift the aesthetics of the hegemonic cultural construct in favour of the 'progressive' allowing the 'space' for other minority narratives.

I conclude that only proletarian revolution can achieve the conditions for an 'authentic' literature as Leon Trotsky argues in *Literature and Revolution*:

> Under Socialism, Literature and art will be tuned to a
> different key such as disinterested friendship will be
> the mighty ringing chords of Socialist poetry. However,
> does not an excess of solidarity, as the Nietzscheans
> fear, threaten to degenerate man into a
> sentimental, passive, herd animal? Not at all. The
>
> powerful force of competition this, in bourgeois society,

> has the character of arket competition, will not
> disappear in a Socialist society, but, to
> use the language of psycho-analysis, will be
> sublimated, Art then will become the most perfect
> ethos for progressive building of life
> in every field.
>
> Leon Trotsky (1981). p 60

The Beat writers could not vanquish 'Moloch', (Capitalism) but they disrupted what Lyotard calls its 'meta-narrative' creating the conditions for 'micro-narratives'. Only proletarian socialist transformation as understood in the aesthetic writings of Trotsky can create authentic liberation. I read Ginsberg as a disappointed Maxim Gorky lapsing into mysticism with juxtaposition of the 'angleheaded hipsters' in Part 1 with 'Moloch' only relieved with fifteen iambs in one 'long-line' without punctuation except the insistent exclamation marks after each Holy! (*Footnote to Howl,* p 27). Ginsberg 'beatifies' poetic language in the hope of a new Communist International to resurrect Trotsky's Fourth International:

> Holy the Fifth International!
>
> Ginsberg, p. 28.

Bibliography

Althusser, L (2006) *Lenin and Philosophy and other essays*, Dahl: Aakar Books.

Adorno, T and Horkheimer, M. ([1944] 1979) *Dialectic of Enlightenment*, trans. by Cumming, London: New Left Books.

Arnold, M ([1869] 1993) *Culture and Anarchy and Other Writings*, ed. by S.Collini, Cambridge: Cambridge University Press.

Asbee, S (2005) The poetry of Frank O'Hara and Allen Ginsberg, Johnston, D (ed) *The Popular & The Canonical Debating Twentieth-Century Literature 1940-2000,* Milton Keynes: The Open University.

Caudwell, C ([1937]1977) *Illusion and Reality*, London: Lawrence & Wishart.

Eliot, T.S. ([1920] 1960) *The Sacred Wood*, London: Macmillan.

Empson, W ([1936] 1966) *Seven types of Ambiguity*, New York: New Directions.

Ginsberg, A ([1956] 2002) *Howl and Other Poems*, San Francisco: City Lights.

Ginsberg, A (2001) *Spontaneous Mind: Selected Interviews 1958-1996.* New York: HarperCollins.

Jackson, A, Modernist Looking: Surreal Impressions in the Poetry of Allen Ginsberg *Texas Studies in Literature and Language, Vol. 52, No. 3, Fall 2010.*
Lodge, J (1972) *20th Century Literary Criticism: A Reader*, London: Longman.

Lyotard, J.F. (1984) *The Postmodern Condition: A Report on Knowledge*, trans, by G. Bennington and B. Massumi, Manchester, Manchester University Press.

MacDonald, D (1953) A Theory of Mass Culture, Rosenberg, R. and White D.W (1957) (eds), *Mass Culture: The popular arts in America*, New York: MacMillan.

MacDonald, D (1962) Against the American Grain, New York: A Da Capo Paperback.

Plath, S ([1963] 2004) *Ariel: The Restored Edition,* London: Faber and Faber.

Ruskin, J (2004) *American Scream: Allen Ginsberg's Howl and the making of the Beat Generation*, Berkley, University of California Press.

Sexton, A (1960) *To Bedlam and part way back,* Boston: Houghton Mifflin Company.

Shakespeare, W (1603) King Lear. Pugh, T and Johnston, Margret R. (2014) *Literary Studies A Practical Guide*, New York: Routledge.

Trotsky, L (1981*) On Literature and Art*, New York Pathfinder Press.

Wordsworth W (1980) Selected *Poetry and Prose of William Wordsworth*, New York: Meriden Books.

Nigel Pearce

The Poetry

Icarus Rising

Nigel Pearce

I am the lost child of Simone de Beauvoir.

"I was made for another planet altogether. I mistook the way."
— Simone de Beauvoir.

An Icarus had flown in the currents that whirl around the disc of
frenzy and Truth,
You were mother half crazed with that music of Beethoven which
caressed minds,
And where else could that Appassionata Sonata be played but bliss
in our heavens,
A wandering Aphrodite chained to a cruel cross, our love was
crucified and bleeds,
Neither of us was for this world, we were made of the stuff dreams
are shaped by.

We celebrated our love of poetry and philosophy, you Muse of past
and the present,
My wings had whipped up a tempest as contorted wings can towards
time so terribly,
Until no longer your butterfly heartbeat for me, but drowned in a sea
of golden coins,
An ornate veil hid a petrified perfection, that brute had finally bought
and formed you,
Mind melts and blood runs sour since there is no sacred milk to
nourish nor heroin hit.

I, amphibian without wings, gliding, sliding through endless pages of
waves and books,
Solitary creature shunned by the world, hermit in a watery
wasteland, thesis and writing.
.

Autumnal.

This season of mellow fruitfulness the apples were teeming with termites,
That Tree which held a fruit of temptation called knowledge is now rotten,
An earth where its roots clasp and grasp is frozen like leaden bronze sky.

A howler of hurricanes tossed the loose leaves; laughter was lost so soon,
This woman who kicks her way through the shades of brown and crimson
Until she flees in a flurry of rustling colour, Eve escapes the Garden gladly.

An Adam lies in depths of a cider vat; he had waved, drunk and drowned,
The leeches replace manacles on his mind and his body is now wormed.

So in a Universe where time grinds with the motion of mortar and pestle,
The divine is shrunk into tedium of day and the humane was hammered
In a mould which was made of clay cracked and so broken melted away.

On Lolita - a novel by Vladimir Nabokov.

—

A marauder within her mind was nobody and that anonymity was like a touch of dew,
At trembling dawn she and the book kept safely within her skirts would walk to bathe,
The pool always had to ripple as if its surface was the doorway to pristine otherness.

My friend do not descend into Lethe[1] streams of petrified demonic grotesque I plead,
It has Siberian chill in its tail and that tail will wag any cosmonaut of that spacey ice,
No explorer of subterranean depths can save you from drowning in their Lethe pool.

The river Styx[2] is not to be crossed without consideration unless a total compulsion,
No it is the boundary between me and your animated death, drugs, shopping malls,
They are the same; mind which writhed numbed now, no more poetry but sophistry.

The mind may have been extended, but it was lost on that trip in the stratosphere,
So now she wanders down to bathe in dew with a copy of Emily Dickinson unread,
A book she could have opened and her poems would have been written on pages.

We weep our tears into silk and weave a cocoon fit for both you and Lolita's woes,
We all knew clever men, paid us with love or the pen upon sculptured manuscript,
There are too many like Lolita for who love is as tender as the night without dawn.

---

[1] Classical Mythology: A river in Hades whose water caused forgetfulness of the past in those who drank it, oblivion.
[2] Classical Mythology: This river was the boundary between the world and Hades.

Icarus Rising

A teenage political prisoner is detained on wards x and y during the 1970s.

An older monk on a secure ward also talked of Tim Leary and Che
so we colluded,
The nurse without eyes just a film covered One presumed in
purveyor of darker art,
A poet wrote in metaphor not grasped by those who had embalmed
patients' minds,

Children are born in a bell-jar of discontent but do not worry doctor
has the thorium,
But the clientele spat sputum into cardboard spittoons not emptied
but flung in rage,
So we were hidden on wards with sycophants, faces like brick and
mortar monotone,

A nurse wanted patients to be aborted cherubs of heaven, some
were like banshees,
No one commented until the ritual burial of a demon because things
are hot in a hell,
Just play bingo pleads Janus therapist while he winks towards some
wincing nurses,

No take over the asylum and make it your campus howls that
interned revolutionary,
The patients rise-up like tigers but then the panzer squad prepare a
chemical Cosh,
As electro-convulsive therapy was had by all in the aftermath, the
wires just buzzed,

Not forgotten were those whose deaths in Stammheim Prison left us
with bitter taste,
Bitter is the taste of lemon, lemon is yellow that will colour us if
cancer strikes in liver,
But red will be funeral shroud as jaundiced eyes never glazed by
cowardice of heart.

Nigel Pearce

Poem to lost love.

'An intellectual is someone whose mind watches itself.
I am happy to be both halves, the watcher and the
watched.'
-Albert Camus.

The worms are in her hair and creep like crazy symmetry of slurred
syllogisms,
Her black and translucent pupils are the corridor back into the infinity
of inferno,
The nymphets were left broken like alabaster dolls sacrificed to a
dumb phallus,
Some gathered their skirts and stole the microdots hidden in haste
but now lost,
Camus stands alone a pillar of stone and utters his words of wisdom
but weeps,
Back in sputnik I spin trying to keep the letters of R. D. Laing 'Knots'
on a page,
Tumble into a purple zone through a rose garlanded window etched
in her mind,
Put the harpsichord concertos on again please I love them much
Hermes sighs,
The statue of Camus vaporized, Hermes levitated and we went
weaving waves.

I write these words about those days of dreams and wish my love
not died in vain,
We were children of ether who were not of this world, entombed
within its bounds.
Note.
Hermes was a god of transitions and boundaries. He was quick and
cunning, and moved freely between the worlds of the mortal and
divine, as emissary and messenger of the gods, intercessor between
mortals and the divine, and conductor of souls into the afterlife. He
was protector and patron of travellers, herdsmen, thieves, orators
and wit, literature and poets.

A light-bulb.
(prose-poem).

He sits in a luxurious sea of crimson cushions observing a solitary
light-bulb.
It is suspended, like his mind, by a single cord. This is pulsating
slightly, or so
 it seems; no it is the bulb flickering. The room, it is like being in a
cube of pure
 white, is caressed by fingers of light and shadow. The darkness is
merging into
the dawn which is peeping through green curtains, they are hung on
steel wires
 suspended between two hooks, the Alpha and the Omega. He finds
his feet and
glides around the bulb to discover a yellowing square of plastic, here
is the switch,
 he clicks it off, the bulb is extinguished and so is his mind, its cast
into an ocean of crawling patterns that dissolves into mirrors of soft
wax. He locates the switch again, pushes the button on and the
knowledge of electricity envelopes his awareness, but the dawn lurks
outside, there is the world.
In that place lurk purple serpents with eyes composed of composite
deceptions, ice which burns like the sulphur of hell, flee knowing I
am both ice and in this purgatory perhaps
That torn and twisted red heart you see before is not cold or black, it
beat too much.

Nigel Pearce

A portrait of my dead mother.

You were confined
in this
sorrow,

Standing quietly entrapped
by a
drama,

Whose ivy script
slowly bound
you.

This actress performed
before an
audience,

until weeping,

Her tattered mask
dissolved onto
a stage of dust with whispers of infinity.

Our mime was like an ancient memory,
A text with those tears that burnt.

I light a candle,
it flickers in this night of cobweb.

'what a shame'.

(in a physical heath Medical Centre waiting room).

Ex-psyche nurse wanders in with an inane grin like he is on gin says
'what a shame',
You are lucky your enamel is still in place for the Herr Dentist[3] had
gouged out mine,
Pull your own daisy[4] but you try that one again and any plastic flower
poetry is gone.

Refresh memory on a ward a decade past: 'you will never study
philosophy', I have.
Whoops, the phlebotomist says they cannot take that vial of blood
you handed her,
You clown minus powder and paint; I am not insane say some in
Latin and Sanskrit,

Poor nurse is absent of mind a shame; he is no more than a pain in
a patient's brain.

---

[3] See Sylvia Plath, *Lady Lazarus.*

[4] *Pull My Daisy:* a poem by Allen Ginsberg, Jack Kerouac and Neal
Cassady. It was written in the late 1940s using a Surrealist
technique. One person writes the first line, the other the second, and
so on sequentially with each person only being shown the line
before. Therefore a poem of this nature could not go beyond the first
line if the person had to pull their own poetic daisy.

Nigel Pearce

Caliban is reincarnated as a snake.

A cobra lay dazed and coiled, with glassy fangs he injected waves
of electrification into Molten blobs of wax serpent was sliding in a fog
of disinfectant around suburbia hooded
amber eyes,
they glow.
He hangs without the chains of slavery, which burden that place,
is poisoned by toxicity of blown innocence.   We left the funeral in
boxes,
 Could only free ourselves from the cemetery of echo by escape
to L.S.D. psychosis to amphetamine dependency to heroin addiction,
to organize the proletariat,
to advocate the armed struggle,
to celebrate the sacraments of schizophrenia.
Poets wonder at love that blows like ribbons into infinity',
But write in cauldrons where the purity of Hades is floating.
Let us dissolve demons with poetry (lines for poets trapped in a
ferment of the Inferno).
They pierced us with a ice thorn and claimed it was their crown of
thorns,
No love,
 then write about it, Blisters of fatigue, burn minds and bodies with
their claws of phosphorus,
No love,
then fright about it, Comrades have been driven like cattle stumbling
into the bloody abattoir,
No love, then fight about it, counter-culture dreams drifted into that
deep and dark well of Narcissus,
 No love, then cry about it, Cannot adore because serpentine cobra
had spat into sad eyes and blinded,
No love, then die about it.
Let us dissolve the mocking demons WITH OUR POETRY NOW.

A poem for William Burroughs.

"I saw the best minds of my generation destroyed by madness, starving hysterical naked,
   dragging themselves through the streets at dawn looking for a fix".
   - Allen Ginsberg: *"Howl"*.
Staring streets reflect the voids in your eyes which are mirrors of the squares,
   they exist without the pricking needle easing   chaos; you found the mainline again,
   an embrace like an orgasm burning through a vein, Zen with and without the hassle,
   this Light strikes those chemical cells calling calmly to the soul like the whispered welcome of nothingness,
   The Absurdity is not in these oceans where weeping tranquility tumbles into dreams
for you were dancing into the masquerades of non-being.
   High womb-like peace sleeps, wake, write, weep, fix again.
You survived, died at 83 beause being you; you always 'went first'.

.

Nigel Pearce

Lines in praise of Sappho.

Your heart is aflame like beauty;
With these flowers you garland sacred Helen
Drifting with your bodies and stroking a sultry air of love flowing
between senses,
Your imaginations of flowers wander in groves with humming
Aphrodite of tears,
Your voices are sweet as flutes at dawn the music wrapping your
beloved's body,
In her white linen robes of purity and desire, on Lesbos the Muses
sang with joy,
To wake a verse of bliss and lyres do play, but night still wails the
song of Rhea.
Then Eros had glanced at them and gasped,
I genuflected dumb before this muse who fragmented.

Notes. 1) Sappho was a significant women poet who lived in about 600 BC on the island of Lesbos where she served as a priestess in the temple of Aphrodite. Her poetry was admired in the Greek world but declined in the medieval period, one pope ordering that her poetry should be burnt. Her poems were written mainly, but not exclusively, for her women friends and followers. 2) Helen was considered to be the most beautiful woman in Greek mythology. 3) Aphrodite was the Greek goddess of love. 4) The Muses were the personification of creative and intellectual beauty in ancient Greece. There were nine and all were women. 5) Rhea is described by Robert Graves as sitting in a cave at the beginning of Time like the "inescapable mother". Sadly she saw her children, except for the last which she replaced with a stone, being swallowed by their father Cronus. 6) Eros is a male god of love. He was a wild god who caused chaos by creating irresistible emotions of love between men and women, women and women, men and me, the Greeks admired him because for them love was limitless.

Mother, it is not Maxim Gorky. [5]

Unlike Gorky, the flower of proletarian authorial voice,This poem will not be like his novel

'Mother',

It is 4.30 a.m. again; and descent into Hades has begun because my aged Eurydice is

entrapped,

The Russian dolls within dolls within a mind have to be unscrewed,given a little personal

autonomy,

Orpheus and his *double* Oedipus must descend and cross the river of the Acheron, a river

of woe,

Gorky saw 1917 blossom, so revolutionaries waited for the winds howl, he crisis came it was

calm,

Mother is bewildered in Hades proletariat is dazzled by reflections of commodities in mirrors,

Not writing 'Mother' and no revolution is the Sisyphean burden for those also expelled from a

heaven.

The ferryman, Charon, undying boatman charges each of us Orpheus and Oedipus a fee it

is insanity,

The depths swirl in a twist of whirlpools which are typhoons of the mind, but he has

navigated across,

Madness possess some incarnations of Orpheus as children they were hurled out in

blizzards of acid,

Metamorphosis from Orpheus into Oedipus is ancient like gnawed wormed apple bitten by a

Serpent,

The poet Ovid writes Orpheus abstains from love of women because things went badly for

---

[5] 'Mother' written by Maxim Gorky was considered the prototype or exemplify form of writing informed by how Marxist writing should be; Socialist Realism. Other Marxists argue rather a method which illustrates the process of alienation in capitalism is preferable. This debate was intense in the 1930's and continues to this day.

him 'no'

The pen is numb and weary of the struggle with double-demonization of the mind and body,

Reality tears like shoals of Paraná fish devour a pair of lovers, I weep and the sea, the sea

is crimson.

Two Traditional Haiku.

01
Sun is the fragrance
Of love breathe that sweet scent choke
And live in moonlight.
-
02
Cherry blossom burns
Bright for those it praises weep
We sleep in the frost.

Note
 The essence of haiku is "cutting" (kiru). This is often represented by the juxtaposition of twoimages or ideas and a kireji ("cutting word") between them, a kind of verbal punctuation mark which signals the moment of separation and colours the manner in which the juxtaposed elements are related.
Traditional haiku consist of 17 morae in three phrases of 5, 7 and 5 respectively. Any one of the three phrases may end with the kireji. Haiku can therefore be said to have 17 syllables.
It should also have a kigo (seasonal reference/ literally a season verse picture e.g. cherryblossom = Spring and lunar = autumn). The majority of kigo are drawn from the natural world

The Day I realized René Descartes was wrong.

You were an 'I' who could not pass through the eye of a needle too wealthy in ideas,
That Doubt of dream games of molten wax, but you were not an explorer of Psyche,
An ideologue who would never doubt Cogito Ergo Sum[6] along his preordained Way,
Conjured an Evil Genius to deceive all, the thought of deception without a hesitation,
Squares become triangles in a Cartesian circle, round and round you were just dizzy,
Baseline was always going to be Saint Anselm, the proof of perfection by God alone.

René the rabbits were all in a bag the one you pulled out was Carroll's White Rabbit,
That day my doubt became an epiphany was when the lie of Cartesian Doubt died,
An awaking of a lotus flower in the moonlight, rebirth in the mists of lunacy and love.

---

[6] Cogito Ergo Sum
'I think therefore I am.'

Lines for 'J' (down and out in London).

You, most precious saint of the sacrament from beyond
enlightenment,
We had stalked along the pavements of dust that billowed into our
minds,
Core like mine was pure Zen Void tied to the sacred vein in knots,
A dazed Dionysus with tongue of fire roaring love for our tribe,
Contempt for those swarms of ants that crawl in rhythmic conformity,
Squares within squares, pulsations of electrical energy
Who preyed on us, prayed for us blind to their encrusted corruption;
Beloved jive junkie whose crimson sedition is still shouting from
misty eyes,
Down and up in London, still defying that recurring Obelisk of glinting
black stone,
I hope...

Hippie woman in a North London squat, 1973.

A chick is sitting in silence within the broken shell of
An egg, her radiance ripples around the room sinking into
Beds Of rose petals, now her gaze begins to penetrate
The wall, white light is flickering out of his hollow sockets of nil,
His murmurings are staring, but she moulds that lava surge
Into a river and is deflecting energy into a collapsing circle,
Wrapping her breath in lace

The poet's tasks: a blessing or curse.

Still hard at heel, those steel bonds don't bind his mind like blinkers,
The fire is not to be quenched within his mind and body: a vocation?
Those flames which lick like lovers probing tongues cocoon, wrap
Him,
But they just burn and erode the being, this is the poet's grained
Fate,
No choice almost like a sort of pre-destination of despair, myopic
mass

Regard the art and what remains of the craft as a gift, a blessing.
A poet's pulsating brain, it exists autonomously in an opaque bell-jar,
And is aware of two solutions: firstly the slashing of the wrist, the
filling,
 Of a fountain pen and then exorcism with ancient incantations of
poetry,
The buzz of bliss may rush up his vein and blast the mind into
fragments,

Always a 'come-down' and poet's scribing scribbling will not sustain
sanity.

On Anne Sexton and her fellow "confessional" poets.
(a Shakespearian sonnet).

Her hands began to write a page with dew,
Those hearts had shed the haunts and bonds of light,
She turned and smiled to cast a spell, this guru,
So tense until her pen began to write,
A verse of storms, angels of night that share
Her seas of lavender wept waves of wonder,
The sun had raised so red to kiss her hair,
She sat quite still and breathed like Buddha.
Her wine could sweeten bitter potions
But doctors, priests of modernity,
Were glaring flames, her poems were emotions
They tossed to Hell with shocks of electricity,
This burnt into these hearts of love, the mind
Was numbed by barbiturate and lay blind.

Dreaming of Morpheus and William Burroughs.
(a Petrarchan sonnet.)

We groove along furrows to cut the wet pavement,
This street reflects an inner web, this glassy maze,
The path to oblivion, it melts like an echo of praise,
The temple begins to sing with awaking ferment,
The dream-powder, its magic is like night's scent,
A garden of delight where sight and tears are glazed,
You spike the mainline again; this is not so crazed,
The cobweb is caught like a dream's finite content.
But Morpheus is a cruel god, in darkness confess
His bonds, we know his mellow, like a nocturne
We were naked, our mind's flow to be dissolved,
A cloud whose rain which beats us nails,
Venus Always burns away my colours in eyes not taciturn,
What remains, the riddles of thought, never told?

Six haiku.
 #1.
Rust burnt in a mind
It was acid, now teardrops
Explode euphoric.

#2.
 Corn stood strong golden
 Ready for harvest, the rain
 You brought left famine.

#3.
A heart was made of
Blue glass and beat, but it broke
Smashed like smithereens.

#4.
Madness exhales breath
To lift veils, there the sane gasp
For they have no air.

#5.
Vampire bat poets
Had sucked your veins, gave them blight
The depths they needed.

#6.
Love was spat out like
Spittle, a flute is silent
For it has no reed.

Blood-Jet.

'Poetry is like the blood-jet,
It just keeps on flowing.'
                    - Sylvia Plath .

An Apple[7] was offered by that delightful serpent, she snakes into a syringe as the vein is hit,
Or gushes from the severed artery of a child when hit by shrapnel, seeps from that cut wrist,
Her brilliance is in the ability to transform any piece of cloth from pure white to a darkest red,
She flows through every syllable this severed finger[8] slides across tyranny of the blank page,
She is dripping from the poet's pen in splendid crimson as from a vampire's satiated mouth,
A poet's ink blood is deeper red being contaminated by crazy cells which is lemon cancer,
He had bitten the Apple offered, gorged upon it but it was not in the Garden of Eden but Hell,
The Invisible Gardener[9] had forgotten to give him entry to Eden, the poet fell before the Fall,

---

1 In the biblical account of The Garden of Eden, humanity is damned for partaking of the fruit of knowledge which was an Apple. The Apple is offered to Adam by Eve who plucked it from the Tree of Knowledge. She was thought to have been influenced by 'The Serpent'. This whole narrative/myth is recounted in The Book of Genesis and is called 'The Fall.'
2 William Burroughs, the Beat novelist, severed his finger and then took it in an envelope to his psychoanalyst.
3 The Parable of the Invisible Gardener is a tale told by John Wisdom. It was later developed by Anthony Flew who made a few changes such as changing the gardeners to explorers. It is often used to illustrate the perceived differences between assertions based on faith and assertions based on scientific evidence, and the problems associated with unfalsifiable beliefs. The main point of the parable is that religious believers do not allow anybody to "falsify" their assertions; instead they simply change their beliefs to suit the questioner. This is why for Flew religious believers cause God to "Die the death of a thousand qualifications" The tale or 'thought experiment' runs as follows: "Two people return to their long

Poetry is like the blood-jet, then anaemia leaves these poets prostrate before time of death.

Two Classes, Two Poetics.

A hair and the width of it is all that matters on the scalp because it is seething like greed,
You need trophies because of all those lost like any myopic vulture searching for carrion,
That bejewelled pen you posture with run dry before any ink oozed to awake blunted nibs.

The nib of the masses is forged with both steel and blood, it has the sound of thunder clap,
It writes on papyrus, parchment and paper, the internet and is flexible like a willow in wind,
We have many pens, you know not all who hold them, some scribes, sleepers and workers.

One History, two classes, two poetics and a single struggle: clash of revolution and reaction.

---

neglected garden and find, among the weeds, that a few of the old plants are surprisingly vigorous. One says to the other, 'It must be that a gardener has been coming and doing something about these weeds.' The other disagrees and an argument ensues. They pitch their tents and set a watch. No gardener is ever seen. The believer wonders if there is an invisible gardener, so they patrol with bloodhounds but the bloodhounds never give a cry. Yet the believer remains unconvinced, and insists that the gardener is invisible, has no scent and gives no sound. The skeptic doesn't agree, and asks how a so-called invisible, intangible, elusive gardener differs from an imaginary gardener or even no gardener at all."

Poem of a redeemed suicide.

An angel had fallen into Grace,
this is the damnation at the antechamber of despair,
Now beyond tepid temptations
he stumbles through the scrub of tangled blind stares
Of willful unseeing eyes no blind stares and jealous glares of those
who claim to spare,
This baptism is of sand, a font
of dust just like those who are sieves, nothing there but Barbed wire
and head
holes,
the fruitless bites of those rotten apples makes me puke
Into an abyss which is home
I know it well, here the lotus flower blossoms at 5.00 a.m.
A poet was persecuted by the magicians of modernity the priest
purveyors of psychiatry,
His persuasions are portrayed in patterns of ink which we call words,
not smeared turds.
Their wands are broken on the philosopher's stone which is where
the poets learn craft.

Nigel Pearce

Her Book of Cold Spells.

Moonbeams awake again as the White Goddess2 has crackled into
his mind like electricity,
This morning the pen scribbles because a poet's thighs are bound in
tight bondage of blue,
A witch had locked the belt some barren desert drifting time ago with
her brass prison key,
She peddled tears and fears from a pious silence, her book of
charms only cast cold spells,
The bell had rung at birth to exorcize desire from her body that
perished in pure purgatory,
Curses were cast in her casket; she gouged out hearts with a lunar
crazed cardiac surgery.
To tickle love3 again would not be metaphor, but a rook woman who
writes with dark thread.

Note.
'The White Goddess: a Historical Grammar of Poetic Myth' - Robert
Graves (1948).
Corrected, revised and enlarged editions appeared in 1952 and
1961. The White
Goddess represents an approach to the study of mythology from a
creative perspective.
Graves argues the existence of a European Deity the "White
Goddess of Birth, Love andDeath" similar to the Mother Goddess
inspired and represented by the phases of the Moon who lies behind
the faces of the diverse goddesses of various European and pagan
mythologies. Graves argues that "true" or "pure" poetry is
inextricably linked with the ancient cult-ritual of his proposed White
Goddess and of her son. These ideas influenced both Sylvia
Plath and Ted Hughes.
'If I was tickled by the rub of love' – Dylan Thomas (1934) [extract].
If I were tickled by the rub of love,
A rooking girl who stole me for her side...
I would not fear the apple nor the flood...
And that's the rub, the only rub that tickles.
And what's the rub? Death's feather on the nerve?
Your mouth, my love, the thistle in the kiss?...
I would be tickled by the rub that is:
Man be my metaphor.

The Transformation.

That saint of sanity is trapped in a glass menagerie of sanctimonious deceit,
Until a flea has penetrated the dome and flies around in search of dog dung,
The master of platitudes swipes the irritant into apparent oblivion with a fist,
A metamorphosis takes places and the black dot mutates into a fluttering bat,
Hideous beauty is born it crawls leaving a trail of crimson slime on the floor.
Being blessed with a sound mind the saint books a check-up with Doctor Sane,
The shrink with a grin and a wink says you have found your vocation Narcissus,
To be generous I will diagnose you with schizophrenia so you better play a role,
Go and roll into the foetal position because it is medication time says that nurse,
Insanity's martyr lives in an asylum but it is dwarfed by the shrine of Absurdity

A latter-day leper

A bug was bagged just for moral sanctimony in a shop of a holy sacred music faith,

It was a case of contagion danger so he is to be pillared as he must be on the fiddle.

No nothing to do with appearance for they know not yes they do he has the plague.

I have the flu so have this rather large of box of tissues I bought at Boots just now,

We do not want any of that here they say in a jerked horror which is spattered out,

A leper is not in a colony it is clear but is from an asylum, prison or infections unit.

They are so pleased until the parasite speaks and is sprinkling holy water on them,

Exchange complete, money for folk, manna for Mammon, art thou holy hypocrite,

All are children of the bourgeois so germ smiles and says good-bye and they reply.

This poet in amber begins to weep with ink these words for people cut like knifes.

Another Adonais.[10] (upon the suicide of a friend).

Looked in those eyes and saw a galaxy of stars like death's
untameable love,
Not beloved Cohen's 'bird on a wire' but your words with syllables
unstained,
Tigers glancing out of the shadows but always they would purr
perfect pulses,
Asymmetry maybe but who wants to be a square, disequilibrium of
pure tides,
They would wash us both away into torrents of tremendous terror but
tenderly,
Always the day dawned danced its words across our minds, the
cloud of light.

A scroll not rolled out for those staid sane pens with their soulless
nib scratch,
Our pens etched souls of amber, but words will reverberate like love
and loss.

---

[10] Adonaïs: An Elegy on the Death of John Keats written by Shelley
uopm the death of Keats.

Haiku.

The winter spirit
Smiles, mistletoe whispers but
Always breaks like ice.

Haiku.

This sun shimmered stalks
Of corn pieces wounded flesh
And shed icy blood.

Experimental poem: number 1.

Caressed the echo of a void embraces reverberation,
 Ache descends in a river breaking the clasp of mind.
 Engulfed in the id being tuned for a birthing of primal mother,
She wept with the stroking of acid droplets those have been caught,
These eyes are dissolved with a flickering of colours that is a still pool in the twilight.

Experimental poem: number 2.

Poetry lives in a crystal teardrop,
It is here that worms burrow
Spewing like the earth retching lava,
Clasped by the mind manacles slicing the body into daylight and the darkness,
Night is whispering with her misty breath.

Experimental poem: number 3.

Sand just flows through a honeycomb mind,
 Ideas are blown across an iridescent wasteland,
Dissolving into an ocean of beats, we throb, a pulse with this blood,
Wept in eyes cried for wandering poetry,
Descend into swarms of crawling echoes like the dissonant rhythm
of chaos.

Experimental poem: number 4.

Tied to a stake, this ravishing of fire
 caresses the free thought of the shrouded solitary mind,
 Heretics burn in their emancipation, the purity of our conflagration,
Caresses the cruel laughter of a celebrant who is mocking   us,
We sing in the finitude of our damnation, visionaries, we are
incarcerated in the flames.

Experimental poem: number 5.

White light licks into an abyss with the touch of totality,
The tongue draws a kiss murmuring with redolence,
This is eternity with whispered dew, begin our sobbing like a dried
lake,
The butterfly is caught in morning flight wrapped in a veil, his
temple of mediocrity,
She is beginning to scribe oceans of lemon, here night and its
burning tears are coaxed   into humming, the drowsiness is like
twilight.

Experimental poem: number 6.

The lunar chasm of verse free with association,
Ivy acid dissolving the page into running plagues of caged rats,
Wire trap-door is opening onto the desert   as masks are cast in
rivers of clay,
The smile of a bemused mystic at night, she is writing with those
caustic tears of fire to be entranced in the cloudy liquid of dreams,
spike is eased into the mainline as infinity beckons.

Psychiatric nurse, try reading some Dostoevsky.

The psychiatric nurse wears a smile of roses,
But when he opens his mouth only the thorns
Show, they rip into us as mercury is rising up the
Thermometer, but we are like Mercury, we are
The messengers of words, of communication
Between mortality and the void, our emotional
Temperature is wrong, our perceptions are askew,
So chant the nurses as they prostrate themselves
Before an idol 'THE SELF' in its glory and feel one
Of the few, a mental health professional, we break the
Shackles on the nurse's ego and drag them from their
Shallows of grey bourgeois murk, then of course they
React and start behaving like enflamed flamingos, with
Moments of insight here, incisive understanding there,
And then in wonder a diagnosis: nurse read Dostoevsky
And step into his weird world of underground people.

In the temple of Aphrodite.

Shoot
white light in a rush
to entwine in pulsations with the ivy of death,

drown in that heaving tissue
with our shadows of poetic nothingness,
we are cast into hollows

Here
banshees
awake us from frozen

dreaminess with their folds of white silk,
they sooth our cries

In
temples where those melting molecules are vibrating,
it is here that we weep with Aphrodite.

No more will the creatures of Prometheus fail in their tasks.

A spark zigzags then you put a hand to cool the heat into this lake and your fingers,
Became frost bitten and they just clawed us cruelly, the reaction we pose does not
Require refrigeration rather a transformation from victims of timidity into blacksmiths
Of molten metal, we fashion steel into objects of collective Nemesis, instruments of Retribution; once buried and lost until the new vanguard of Spartacus performs acts,

To lance a swollen abscess of pus, it must be drained, the bare-foot doctors Inflict
A necessary pain an incision, a wound with History's scalpel, poets don't just wear
The masks of Dantesque masquerade, no; our dreadful dream is a relentless beams.

The chess board consists of 64 squares, are you one?

The chipped chess pieces, the pawns, chant their abhorrence at the
Smooth and uninterrupted movement of both a Rook and the Queen,
At the fatal power of the Kings demise which terminates their game,
He was checkmated because of impotence and ineptitude, you didn't
Avoid being mated: the Grand Master who is reincarnated as a flea
Studies the game, metamorphosis's himself into sticky brown slime,
He then oozes onto the board, only godless like the inexorable tides,
The tacky mucus seeps its way into the pristine chequered surface.
Did you lead a chequered life or as cramped as the pawns, chipped
And clipped, never raced from A8 to R8, only P-K4*, an anticipated
Opening and so is everything else, just predictable like the ticking of
A chess clock, you 'play by the rules', 'stay on the board'; secure, its
Death-in-life because the brown snot is caustic, it will erode you until
Deranged the only option is to plead for checkmate, you 64 squares.

The runaway.

Darkness dawned as his swimming sperm and her egg of shell fertilized in eclipsed dance, This wass genesis of the children who tumble in dust of those goblins glared like death,
They impaled these children upon stakes of plastic prepared us to become an adornment
Of bourgeois taste that square whitewashed prison-cell called family,

It begins as they as they hammer those first nails into you   the crucifixion
Iis by white noise, eyes pierced by glass arrows until death comes aged six,
A body wrapped in a shroud of pins,
The child was resurrected at thirteen; he was beginning to plough the lime furrow,
Through fields of lemon, they had folded into a daze of hazy tangerine.

Conception in the desert.

Jab
a silver
pin into any

Poet
and see
sand pours out,

It
flows into
a scratched hourglass

Which
leaks particles
through dream's prism

Into
desert, here
poetry is conceived

With
those relentless
sandstorms, they blind.

Icarus Rising

Elegy for Elise Cowen('beat' poet: 1933-1962).

Your smile is bright with magic, it draws in verse
To glimpse the "straights", their vision is blurred
And gazes inert, that form is carried in a hearse,
But you who danced the naked poetics preferred

The peace of wombs, the warmth, and "rush" induced seductress,
Our wastes are frozen with promises, caught and chosen
This moth of candle and flame is burnt and wingless,
At dawn you're cupped in a wrinkled hand and have written

A dirge of deserts and biting sand which sings
Into the syringe, enchantment of the finite "fix"
Lies with accusations on pages scribed in blotted rings,
This sacred insanity is vibrating your soul, a matrix

For jewels the wind whispered opiate kiss, its
In here where belief lies on the periphery, the poetry
Ascends in grace with those from Auschwitz,
You stumble across the graveyards and weep in symmetry.

On poets who lose their sanity because of unrequited love.

Love
had sweetened tongues
to caress in these dreams of bliss,

Numbed,
this night is enclosed in a cell.
the shadows of desired,

Emptiness gaze from the melancholy in her eyes,
the poet is cursed by his plague of blindness.

Winter Haiku.

Ice has formed across
A lone pool, words are crying
Beneath its smooth face.

Haiku written in memory of Edie Sedgwick (1943-1971).

Bliss was fixing fire
 In shadows, flower of flame
 You wilted to bloom.

Haiku on poets

Cut that mind of coils
 And it bleeds an ink of joy
 That is caught by stars.

Haiku No. 4.

A pillar of stone
Has a cloak of golden
It wraps itself in.

A poet becomes catatonic.

A
heart of dust
is fleeing the square of black onto white,

The
silken veils are drifting into a river of mirrors,
here baptism is transience trapped in a house of tears

With
the Dead, they kiss with burning words
like bubbling acid which blisters until poetry is left mute.

A priest realizes God is dead and mourns.

A chill
chasm of coldness
is beating this heart

Where
once lover's warmth
had ridden like dawn,

He
had celebrated
a mass, a libation,

Now
standing stunned
in torn vestments

Night
has enfolded
his soul, the sacrificial

Rite
of Winter frost
has frozen his tears into rivers of ice.

Nigel Pearce

Lines on the loss of love.

The poet had gazed into a sky of lime green clouds carved
In crystal, his mind embraced a sun of white linen, but her
Sun sunk and spiralled before him into a world without those
Who love to roam the lunarscape, there poets fix into dream,
That stratosphere is where the fallen angels who touch mind
And body perform their undying ballet of love and lamentation.

The poet's moistened eyes can see only her drama of pain,
He genuflects before her bejewelled chalice, but its wine has
Seeped into luminous gutters, here the drunken poets tumble.

Metamorphosed.

A crown of thorns is encircled by a ring of rose petals,
Its rays are piercing his eyes of confusion, she sits still
And listens to the foaming breath which winds around
Her head like a black serpent, it is contracting, she is
Suffocating but pulls at the coils of this twisting snake
And begins to heave and then breaths again, he pulls at
The cord and drags it down around his waist in silence,
He's waiting until the black backed beetles have scuttled
Across their dappled floor, she now begins her chant, a
Dirge to gods of dust and lace good-byes, an exorcism of
Insects, she is metamorphosing and flies out of a window.

Nigel Pearce

Narcissi and Red Roses.

Gusts of wind are howling around this white cube,
Our bare room; I pluck the veils of silver cobwebs
From these shrouded, stinging and bloodshot eyes,
A globe of green satin is rolling around the floor in
A mist of purple, at its burning core is a priestess of
Aphrodite, one of those who serve the cult of love
On Lesbos, the isle where Sappho sings her spells.

She begins to celebrate mass, I genuflect before her
Altar of withered narcissi, an aroma of sandalwood
Is weaving like dust blown across a calm sea, this
Scent intoxicates our senses, my supplicant's hands
Are cupped in the form of a chalice before her, she is
Peeling the petals from a red rose, they flutter gently
Into a porcelain cup, it shatters into jagged fragments.

Our Lady of Sorrows in Notting Hill Gate (1974).

That green-scaled goddess of grief how she is wailing from her
  Brown soil grave, it is here that those recently resurrected Dead
Exchange their laughter without lament,but you, who are skeletal
With yellow skin pulled tight in a smile of delight, you, a beatified
Courtesan who roams these connected and tuned-in grids, a
                                heart
Wrapped in the sackcloth which is worn by an incipient lover of
Chaos, here a frozen embryo begins to pulsate, it breaths and
                                stings
    The bitter pulp of that apple bitten in the Garden of Pleasure,
                            ice folds
Into our eyes until lost we're born into this spectrum of zoned
                            silence,
    I embrace you, you are taking the crucifixion from my eyes,
                          we weep.

.

Nigel Pearce

Oedipus is expelled from Eden.

Her tears of crystal are an unbound metaphor dripping
From those silent pools of his mother's ocean of eyes,
Oedipus glances away, blinded with pain, picks-up a
Syringe and finds his mainline to a tranquillity of night,
In these depths there is a shadow dance of desire and
Oedipus is tied to the mast for this voyage into a zero,
Sirens, lovers, mothers and the Madonna are the poetry,
Their nectar is sweet to taste, his tongue touches moist
Petals and caresses with the relish of finite whispering.

But the Inquisitor gazes down spewing us from an Eden,
We were beatified with a band of light around our heads,
But a bond of thorns is formed which pierces both mother
And son, they now roam an interminable lunar wasteland.

Hymn to the Mortality of the Nazarene.

The Void beckons like graves welcome the dead,
She weaves barbed threads of wire, dark mystery,
To coronate the poet who paces forward to glance
Into an infinity of broken glass, her eyes of smiles
In circles of black staring from a bed of rippling folds,
Here she washes the blood from sheets, these stains
Are bled in a cycle of betrayal and love, sunset and
Sunrise, he wipes the tears of mortality from his eyes
And steps to look beyond the edge, a taunting precipice,
He howls "Father, Abba, why did you leave my corpse to
Hang among unclean men and these anaemic women"?
"Mother, why wasn't it your blood which mingled with the
Blood flowing from my wounds in hands, feet and side?
You blessed the wisdom of fools, that myopia of deserts",
This infant, the Lamb, is a man tuned into those pulsations
f Alpha, he leaps into the Void to dance with the damned.

Psalm to the poetry of joy.

The moon rises like mist distilled from a burnt river
To whirl with her humming until the bonds unravel,
Now she is caressing her smile into radiant morning,
Her dust is lingering it sprinkles onto dormant souls
Of night awaking our song of love to a golden dawn,
The poet's pen is dipping into this chalice of nectar,
We wander across pages with infinity and innocence
A dance with the light and shadows of sacred ritual,
Psalm of joy to a pristine moon and the drowsy sun.

She is the bridge across the river of Death.

A vulture sweeps on hidden currents seeking carrion. We cuddled death and squeezed it out of a rock; the vibes began gliding around a hill of lush green grass overshadowed by
A Gold Phallus,
The phallus ejaculated the words of the dull with a force that shot them high into the
sky where glazed eyes are blind, drilled them into the side of the head where dilated
pupils are gobbling madness into their depths and then a pink fish gulped their dirge.

Flying beyond the cruel clasp of fire and reaching the icy shady spheres where there
was a river of sparkling glass which was fluid and flowed fast, a woman clothed with black robes approached, her face was deathly pale and her eyes dark and sad, she said: 'take my hand', we floated on and skimmed across the surface of the river that sparks,
her whisper is melody: 'this is your end, dissolve atom by atom in my tunnel of night'.

Nigel Pearce

The Broken Mirror.
(a journey into the subconscious of the poet.)

Those eyes of a mistress at dawn cloaked in silence,
Staring into the hollow vision of his sight like night,
The poet, ancient like crazed Oedipus cast in marble,
Burn with those licking flames melting these colours,
Sucked into this still lake of mirrors, wind blows the
butterflies in this star gazed flight, now we are
ebbing into tactile darkness soothed by dusty lunar
wandering.

This mirror is shattered by the incessant beating with hail,
ost clad poetry swallows glass, we're stumbling Adams.

Dreaming of the Muse.

On Poetry
sweetest tears are wept,
Caressing the shadows of silence
this Muse is ancient as Electra;

She whispers breath onto a
tissue psyche,
Which vibrates like a web
of gossamer:

Dream with shifting sands
like a vortex of voids.

Doves with broken wings
who fly from a cage,
Scribe those poems of Night
which ache with love's sorrow.

Nigel Pearce

Prometheus lives just outside of Babylon.

                                              echo
                               baby
                  groover
Babylon
dreamer,
                  drowsy
                               demon
                                              fixing
                                               with
                        Prometheus
              bound
     in
     her
              silken
                        lemon
                                     robe.

The writing of verse with night.

The poet of night's desert begins to scribe
like waves into an ocean whose mist is without dawn,

Drifting across these fields with wonder, like the touch
into swaying seas of corn and sun, sigh with the lovers

Like oceans, their caress is dripping like wax and
breath
onto paper flowers, swirling into an endless spiral of
clouds.

Moonshine weeps into this ocean of nothingness, the
dust
is like a masquerade which is dissolving into white
and zero,

Their masks melt, softening into visions like the
oblivion
with eyes shining, shadows like insomnia with
dreaming.

Spring's dancers wander across the virgin page
with its sighing,
this is a word beginning to form into a wave, a
whisper of sand,

The cloaked pen weaves into this morning shimmer
of cobwebs
in which the Muse hangs suspended like eternity
cloaked in ivy.

Nigel Pearce

Poem without a title.

No
existence
without language
no journeys
without those words
to
Prepare
self
for
this trip
in
imagination
A
voyage
deep
below
Dive
into
the Abyss
that underworld
it is here that we write with our demons.

The Steppenwolf.

A wolf wanders the Steppes in a dance of solitude,
The deserts of snow stretch interminably, glistening
Expanses without a horizon, his eyes are burnt by
Rays of sun which burrow into a heart woven of silk,
Freedom is the price paid for his emancipation, this
Escape into a wasteland is anonymous, tracks left
Soon melt for he leaves no mark, the only mark is
The one that cuts his heart and from which there is
no escape.

Nigel Pearce

Two poets contemplate Salvador Dali: 'The Persistence of Memory'.

Her mind is opening
like a lotus flower stung

By a spear of steel,
her breath drifts in lemon

Globules, pupils are fixed
on the door which is woven

From willow branches, he
opens an aperture to discover

A zone which interacts
with her black eyes, leaden

By the mist of lunar storms
they embrace, bodies are like

Cotton pages blown across a sea
covered in silver scales, until wrapped

In a ball of silk they exhale rhythmically
with the pulse of the Earth, the clock faces have melted.

To Oblivion.

That mistress with melancholia
is sitting like a consumed Buddha
in my prison cell,

Holy tears are wept dry here
descending into a fathomless verse,
Feel the breath

but never the caress of her soul,
Intimate with the finite of vacuums
whispered like night.

The Inquisitor pierces this haven
with voids
Melting our eyes

of glass which are pristine with weeping,
Footprints in the sand are swept away in
waves of oblivion like spirals of hollow.

To Art.

The Void, its cloud has rain,
A spring to quench our sight,
To damn and pierce the pain,
But art is fire in flight.

Lines written in melancholy.

Sweetest death
you are the goddess of summer nectar,
The honey for the poet to drown in unconsciousness,
verse is prostrated before you, both in mind and body:
Holy One,
Holy Oblivion,
Holy Death.

We, the children of the soul's catacombs scribe our ink
onto virgin paper,
The white page glances shyly, trembles a little,
anticipating the pen,
A nib begins to weave tapestries of willow meaning,
these are cloaked in the shrouds of images floating along a stream,

we are wandering through this labyrinth of poetry.

Dylan and Caitlin Thomas drink themselves into oblivion.

Let us dance with our dream of death,
Grasp tightly together, tumble in tunnels
Chanting to nil, to cloaked zero, to chaos,
Until freed from this frenzy of whirling fire
We're stroked into sleep, a slumber of solitude.

The ice-box.

This is a box within a box, a world within a world, a house which is typical of many found within suburbia. It is brown bricked, anonymous and almost transmits hymns of praise to some tarnished copper god of mediocrity. In the kitchen of this house stands a fridge, it looks white and prosaic. Open the fridge door and at the top on the right is a sky blue ice-box, it has three white stars to confirm the adequacy of its freezing capacity. Inside the ice-box is a rectangular tray which is divided into squares, each can be filled with water and then frozen to produce the perfect ice-cube. This can then be dropped into a frosted pink glass which wraps around it, add fruit juice and there is the perfect chilled drink.

A son frequently opens the fridge door and pulls down the sky blue ice-box flap and peeps inside. He examines the frosted walls which, paradoxically, burn his fingers; they are almost burnt with the coldness. It is in this world of ice-cubes that he discovers another dimension which exists separately from, but is intrinsically attached, to the ebb and flow of everyday life. The son had an unusual relationship with the ice-cubes in the fridge finding great comfort in popping two out from the tray and holding them in his hands until they were numb and the ice-cubes dissolved into water.

The living-room of this box within a box was bare, no carpet, no furnishings or pictures. However glaring at him was a gas fire. It had short brown steel legs with one at each end to support it. A copper pipe stuck up through the floor boards and was connected to the fire. The fire itself was coloured in two tones of brown, light-brown at the bottom and around the sides of the gas jets and above was dark brown. The shelf which was on top of the whole apparatus and rested against the wall had white plastic knops at each end, one is to turn-on and ignite the gas and the other is to control the flow of gas in order to regulate the temperature. This fire concerned the son greatly, it almost dominated him. He didn't like the hissing of the gas or the flickering flames and the brief smell of gas at ignition caused him much anxiety. He felt little or no choice but to constantly check and check again that the gas was burning correctly and there was no leak. With the certainty of the tides his life became enslaved to this gas-fire. The only respite was allowing the ice-cubes to melt in his hands.

Just as the season's motion is inevitable the gas fire developed a leak. Fortunately the son was elsewhere when the explosion tore through the house destroying it and its anonymity. It no longer looked like all the other houses in the cul-de-sac. The fridge was badly damaged and thought to no longer fulfil any useful task; it was taken to the local tip. The ice-cubes turned into water, but a more profound metamorphosis took place: a voice said:

'My son, there is no longer any need to worry.'

The water had leaked from the ice-box and out of the fridge into the rubbish of the tip in which it germinated a seed planted at the beginning of Time. The shoot will push its way up through the waste and bloom next spring, a snow-drop.

The tale of a mother and her son.
(a narrative poem).

Prologue.
In our beginning was pitch, infinite darkness,
There Isis conceived this sun-dazzled Icarus,
Isis, my mother, fountain of spring and winter's
Frozen wasteland, you wept me into a genesis,
It was here we feasted on the rotten fruit which
Fell from the Sacred Tree, then staggering drunk
With love and hate we embraced clouds of gold,
We settled on the boarder of this chiming Garden,
Our dance was performed before the silver Serpent.

Wanderers of the psyche.
Mother, a Jewess of the soul rather than the blood
Grasped my hand and guided me from the Garden,
There the Serpent's tongue had licked shut our eyes,
We roamed hazy peaks and caverns of biting dreams
Until this child was cast in a mould, set, yet still molten
With lava which spewed from the Fall's ancient volcano,
This river burned furrows in our minds, two souls which
Had journeyed alone were one in the fire, like intoxication
We wandered with Psyche, she who is unfathomable love.

Icarus soared.
The awakening screwed into this sun-dazzled Icarus,
I wept as mother entered the labyrinth of dazed lies,
Leapt out of that snare, the trap of enclosed terror and
Focused on the poetry of psychedelia and joyfulness,
Visions I saw in the sky and soul whispered into the sun,
I soared and caressed the gaze of a Serpent of silver
In suspended heaven, there waxen eyes were melted,
Dripped, drop by crystal drop into a sea of frosted glass
To freeze the milieu of those "straights", they follow zero.

Mother dies.
The black clams of Time stuck onto mum's frail body,
Those rusty chains of age and illusion bound her mind,
She spiralled inwards in an introspective frenzy of sparks
As her autumn leaves were blown into the chill of winter,
I walked with her and her ghosts in that becalmed odyssey,
Slimy sea monsters would rise and frighten us, both
children,
Mum and I would sit in the house of dementia, she sat
hunched
And meditating on the coloured interwoven threads of her
memories,
Until the wind blew her, that crumpled paper Buddha, away
into infinity.

Prose-fiction.

A modern psychomachy[11]

A troubled and largely sleepless night and Peter the priest scuttles like a frightened beetle out of his shell of reverie. His dreams are becoming a little too intense and seem to merge into wakefulness. The priest slumps beside the bed and prays:
'Holy Mother of God, the habit is returning, I beg you
Blessed Virgin, I've got to give it up'.

His skin is no longer young, not a fresh page on which to scribe poetry to the grandeur of God who had been his fountainhead in the early years. Alternatively it is not the wrinkled criss-crossed dried parchment of an old man awaiting his wake. His prayers seek solace in the Christ of the sacrament he celebrated at Mass daily.
'Jesus of the Holy Blood I need a hit of you like that first time I celebrated the Holy Mass, what joy, unadulterated beauty. '

It had been over three years ago when he read Goethe aloud at an evening with some close priest friends from those spring sweet scented blossom seminar days. Father Liam had played a jig or two on his battered and scratchy violin. Those notes had pieced Peter's side like a knife and he had bled poetry:
'Two souls, alas, are housed within my breast,
and each will wrestle for the mastery there'.
'Yes, Father Peter, Goethe again, very good and all well when we were novices, but we're ordained priests.'
'I had noticed that Father Pious.'
'Come come, poetry and Father Pious' sherry.' smiled Father Liam.

He knew the others had looked-up to him in those days, but they were so staid except for Liam, not of the 'Kingdom of God'. But something snapped that night, a 'dark night of the soul' had engulfed Peter.

His understanding of what was meant by the immaculate had been transformed; indeed body and soul were transmogrified almost like that quivering melody which caressed him from Liam's violin.

Immaculate blood had meant only in the silver chalice he raised with extreme care to a line above his forehead for his meagre bunch of communicates to genuflect before. His parish had been mainly hypocrites and deceivers, a real bunch of Pharisees. One or two he had high hopes for like 'madman John':

---

[11] The term psychomachy comes from a Latin poem 'Psychomarcia' (c400BC) by Prudentitrusabout the battle for a person's soul. In the Medieval period they were dramatized as 'morality plays.'

No reason you cannot fulfil your vocation to the ideals of Saint Francis of Assisi.'

John had begun shoplifting and giving away stolen-goods to those street-addicts in the poor quarter.

Yes that was a place for a priest to minister, but not to have their brown and white powders and those hellish off-white crystals administered to madman John or anyone else. He'd genuinely believed then the flock at Mass were different to those skeletal, emaciated creatures with taunt yellowing shin pulled around sunken eyes, those deep black hollows, those empty eyes, my God.

Peter quickly pulls on his baggy black priestly uniform which covers and gives some volume to a meagre frame, the rest he explains by his devotion to fasting. But then the cold burrows, almost bits, like a pulsating, squirming pile of purple worms and claws, eats into his body which would whiplash intosome kind of sweat that seemed like a tropical fever. He knew that the mainline to the Divine is not theone recommended by his spiritual director, who he assiduously avoids, but the immaculate track which is marked by those stigmata which were nothing but regular neat lines of needle marks. Mass was at six fifteen, he needs to straighten-out for that, but he could not celebrate that Mass for those who attended so early where the real zealots and had the suspicions of your average drug-squad officer. What was the remedy? He knew only too well, it smashed through his skull into that tormented brain, of course there was nothing to worry about; he had stashed a little 'brown' away and with a couple or

three tablets of diazepam he would be fit again, perhaps not to celebrate the Mass, but manage some kind of automated performance without his fingers becoming appendages of his hands fiddling feebly and trembling in a fumble out from his vestments.He rummages under the sink, thank God, here's the stash. Unravel the brown paper in a flurry of

hands, yes here's all that's required, praise be to whom, he wonders to God or to the 'man'? Suddenly Peter is disorientated no need to worry about 'madman John' he'll get through okay. Disengaging from the surroundings the priest thought he'd fall back into the tedium of the business at hand and it will be soon be Easter. Peter, with the precision of a locksmith, smoothed the silver paper, manoeuvres withthe assistance of a razorblade a line of brown powder that within a minute or two will sooth the creases from his mind. The 'line' of brown powder is straight down the middle of the foil which he holds left handed. A cone had been inserted into his quivering lips, constructed of silver foil, lovingly three years ago. It is now fashioned by his claw like fingers into a utensil of pleasure no more than an instrument of

necessity. In his right hand is an orange plastic lighter. He raises the left hand which holds the foil to within about four centimetres of the cone, ignites the lighter, a click, and with the swift yet careful cigarette...warmth engulfs his mind, then a womb-like peace enshrouds him. Finally he exhales stumbles and sits down.

'Not the mainline to the divine, but it will be adequate until later on.' Peter sighs aloud.

The tumbler of water is lifted, the three yellow tablets of diazepam swallowed.

'Give me half an hour and I'll be steady as the rock upon which the Church

is built.' He whispers playfully.

A series of waves which are like frenzied screeches resound through his mind: madman John how are you, where are you, who are you? He is startled and gathers his paraphernalia

agitatedly, but with the paradox of addiction smoothly into the plastic bag which he places

and wraps in brown paper, then his stash is safe.

Mass then passed fairly uneventfully, a combination of him being 'comfortably numb' and the single track spirituality of the 6.15ers who knew the Mass so well it was less a ritual than a memorized piece of text which they'd pattered out for years, a sort of rapid mindless muttering. These acts of evasion;

these deceptions were becoming more grotesque day by day he thought.

John, who had in many ways Peter pondered was the incarnation of the Franciscan ethic plus; plus what? The psychiatric nurses who would periodically whisk him into what remained of the local mental hospital, much of it lay derelict; care-in-the-community, seemed John didn't receive any 'meaningful' care, at best Peter would use the term management to describe it. What care did either of them really get, but chemical care? Then it hit him, he was beginning to withdraw. Had to get downtown and quickly to the market square and those familiar black clams of shame were beginning to attach themselves to his mind, would people realize he was going out to 'score'. The leeches of an unforgotten passion were

sucking his moist flesh, he must forget:

Father, Father Peter, stop its John. I've been baptising near the river. I'm John the Baptist.'

Holy shit thought the priest; he's really lost it this time and I need a hit.

Don't worry Father it's not full immersion, I'm 'doing them up' with pharmaceutical diamorphine.'

'Thank God.'

'It will soon be Easter Father, so I thought we'd better resurrect

some of those downtown Lazarus people. St. Peter told me himself. You yourself Father Peter. '

'John you child, I'm not a saint, I'm a junkie.'

'We have the immaculate hit; I've got the ampoules here.'

'Perhaps there is something of Peter in me; I've denied my Master more than

three times. There is no mainline to paradise John, we make that or not here on Earth and that is a dreadful burden, an awful freedom. John, let us drink deeply from the streams within our hearts.'

'What about the ampoules Father, why waste them.' John said.

A wry smile came over the gaunt face of the priest and exposed his yellow teeth:

'Well one for the road, just to say good-bye to it all.'

They were found with the blood congealing in their syringes. It was simple; they had forgotten to reduce

the dosage for this was pharmaceutical heroin, not Lazarus gear and there would be no resurrection.

Father Liam's violin had indeed played a drowsy melody to Peter, one that left him in the pleasuredome, but would with an irresistible and remorseless logic which left him a prisoner chained in the dark dungeons of addiction. Liam now has to hide the violin-case with fearful haste.

A Steppenwolf breathes the morning air.

"My mind hums hither and thither with its veil of words."
— Virginia Woolf, The Waves.

The steppes had been a wasteland of significance for the Steppenwolf and some wolf packs probablyhad revenged his mind and body when he had the misfortune to meet them: learning his nature andaccepting   on the savannahs and avoiding those marauding packs had been an important step after many false ones. The other place had its own deprivations that was where they the Worldings lived withall their concerns about banalities; no the Steppenwolf preferred the meaningful desolation and hadbecome habituated to the solitude. For didn't he have his books and writing materials. Whether he had been born here he had wondered much, if he had be born atoll seemed debateable at times after a particularly protracted and lonely trek when a younger wolf of the steppes. They had been a male wolf, from whom he often fled. and another called his 'mother'. The mother had taught him
the ways of the steppes, herself a Steppenwolf but one made captive and taken to a cave where shewas taught to speak like a Worlding but could never quite manage their language of platitudes. But,being of a similar nature, if tamed and harnessed she taught him to listen to the winds which sweptacross the steppes and interpret its beauty, understand its music. The tamed Steppenwolf also taught him to record the Steppes and the World in his notebooks and fashion them into poetry and prose and a love of sniffing that sharp morning breeze and opening a book.As I observe this surreal world I shall not deceive you with his dialogues, his life is an interior monologue which from time to time others are granted access, but his observations of you and yes you are penetrating; you cannot escape those drowsy amber eyes. This world is not the physical world of Central Asia, the Steppenwolf has two rather than four legs yet it is not the green and pleasant land of those cursed with the fidgeting of the sane terrain, no this land is named by some mental illness, by others who believe, although this is by no means certain, they have a privileged knowledge of the
Steppenwolf: 'Paranoid Schizophrenia.' But my acquaintance with him is one of The Omniscient Eye,not divine but one of narrator of tales, the weaver of words.Steppenwolf was 'born to be wild' and as less the fully developed wolf was hitching down the M1,
destination Notting Hill Gate. Not yet the playground of the less than totally sophisticated children of thedollar it was then a British version of Height-Ashby. First 'lift' was off a lorry driver, quite a large articulated one, that is the lorry rather than the driver who was a pleasant man of late middle-age:

Nigel Pearce

'Want a lift, how old are you?'
The Steppenwolf was dressed in kaftan, jeans and beads and with a tee-shirt. He did not reveal the ageof his body, but rather his mind.
'Come on get in, when did you last eat.'
'Like, is that meaningful man.'
'Here take my packed-lunch.'
'Thank you.' the young wolf replied for the steppes he had grown-up in where suburbiaIn fact the exodus to that part of London had in the preceding years been mainly one from affluent ifstifling zones. Like the people of the Book of Exodus these young people believed themselves to beboth blessed and as a consequence persecuted. all believed themselves to comprise a sort of tribe of steppenwolfs, but some were Steppenwolfs amongst the tribe, indeed would wander through magic doors endlessly with and without any assistance, no would rather tumble through them, indeed for this

Steppenwolf he would walk like a somnambulist through doors and entrances and fall over precipices. At first he had not realized people will push you through doors and hurl one over the cliff edge. He had thought at this behaviour was confined to the land of the Worldlings. How wrong can a young wolfsetting out across the steppes from a world of yelling and threats, those are merely transformed into different matter, there can seem to be only dark matter at times, but he possessed the key to shut the doors both magic and otherwise and allow the illusion of existence to be retained. The key to freedom was the written word and the word read in a relationship with the reader however anonymous that may be.

Five years later and the wolf was wandering the plateau with a haversack and the light of the moonfor guidance, the pleasures of the lunar night which are enchantment and torment each in full measure,balanced pecariously like a set of scales suspended from the cloud where the memory of the trail ofSocrates and the his death with a dose of hemlock are pervasive. He was an outcast but did not realizeit, had embraced Harry Hiller, the Steppenwolf of Hermann's novel, as a young man but of course Harry Hiller was a middle aged man when he walked through the magic door and did not have an assortment of brightly coloured phials chained around his mind, oozing into the textures of his brain. Cast out of the wolf pack for he was a little to 'wordy' for many and not willing to act out the correct role of an albino in

the specimen room for eloquent steppenwolfs. The Steppenwolf did not pursue the tarnished calve ofhedonism nor could he be a shepherd for lost sheep or a matador to slay the Minotaur. He slept onpeople's floors and in those old crumbling Trogon Horses, the lunatic asylums. The Steppenwolf was huddled on a park bench, the Worldings eyeing weary for its was a scorching summer's day and

97

he was ensconced in a filthy duffle coat and a very long purple and white scarf wrapped several times around his neck, almost a sort of vestment. He was elsewhere for he was the protagonist of not one but all of Camus' novels; this was a little difficult to grasp. no certainly his mother hadn't died that morning and he hadn't experienced any kind of existential self-realization, but on that bench, day past day past day but 'The Outsider' seemed to have the clarity of a million sunrises with the dew hanging on the whispering grass. Was he Meursault, he wondered: a man of around sixty always walked his Scottish terrier through the park, past the human debris which was the Steppenwolf,

by this time the odour emitting from him must have been fairly potent and have looked rather unkempt?

'My name is Monsieur Meursault and am experiencing

an existential crisis, are you acquainted with this.'

'Bloody hell, he's flipped.' and the dog yapped in

agreement.

The police came and the ambulance and the nurses 'specialed', not allowing even to the toilet byhimself. He refused to take off the duffle coat and the other patients and then the staff called him Paddington. He had a marmalade sandwich just after medication time brought by a Spanish nursingauxiliary Francis with a mug of Horlicks. The Steppenwolf wondered whether Francis was really Italian and from Assisi. Then a young nurse who looked like Rupert Brooke told him quietly:

'If you want to leave, you must stop this high-fluting conversation, then the doctors will think you are better. And for god's sake stop quoting from

'Dust' by Rupert Brooke'

'But it is more than existence, it has essence, it gives life and death.'

He opens the book and read the lines he knew by heart:

'When the white flame in us is gone,

And we that lost the world's delight

Stiffen in darkness, left alone

To crumble in our separate night;

When your swift hair is quiet in death,

And through the lips corruption thrust

Has stilled the labour of my breath --

When we are dust, when we are dust! --

Not dead, not undesirous yet,

Still sentient, still unsatisfied,

We'll ride the air, and shine, and flit,

Around the places where we died,
And dance as dust before the sun,
And light of foot, and unconfined,
Hurry from road to road, and run
About the errands of the wind.
And every mote, on earth or air,
Will speed and gleam, down later days,
And like a secret pilgrim fare
By eager and invisible ways...
'Stop that immediately or there will be a nice little jab for you.'
The 'conditioned reflex' had been taught and 'reinforced' so many time he knew what your hospitalexpects every patient to do, no it was going over the top in a Flanders field to the rat tat-tat of gunfire,but the sound of breaking glass, the struggle and the jab of chlorpromazine. Pre-ordained, conditionedand stamped...

It was a cloud swept rain biting day Father was buried.
It was a cloud swept rain biting day Mother was buried.
The Steppenwolf has carefully arranged his rather abundant supply of medication in colourful piles in sequence of potency in order to make sure the clock stops. But unlike one Paddington Bear, he has cast off the civilising death giving effects of that green and pleasant land or rather the supervised walks around the green and pleasant grounds of those old hospitals and returned to 'darkest Peru' or in his case the metaphorical Steppes of his mind, he is totally alone: emotionally, intellectually and creatively and with the exception of the odd visitor physically. The choice is his, he listens to the Beethoven piano concerto No.5, the one the captive steppenwolf played endlessly in her cave to him, she had tuned him into the music of the crashing spheres, taught him to interpret it and hear it in the cold winds which
sweep across those steppes and given him a key to unlock Pandora's Box but to see that it contained the good, those things he must live and write about. He tidies away the medicines and begins to write. It is 5.00 a.m. on the eighth anniversary of his mother Isis' death. The Steppenwolf goes outside and breathes the morning air and it is good. ,

The night becomes darker: being 17.

This child had been expelled from a womb, aged 7, during the "summer of love". The place, where he had lived was without love, a place of darkness, a matrix of oppression. In this place the glare of intimidation was the god and the angels lived in fear of another deluge of threats. These places, are dark places. He does not know why, perhaps it is just in the nature of these places? Ten years had passed in a whirl of tempest and fear. He had sought sanctuary in the company of souls who did not yell at him, his new companions did not have the strut of oppression and welcomed this outsider into the company of dreamers, in this place he felt safe, these people where not branded with the iron of hypocrisy. They kissed him with potions, wondrous white powders which beckoned him into a world of meaning and caring. Initiating him into a world of compassion and the poetry of oblivion, they prepared his fix. The pristine white powder floats into a spoon, a lighter ignites, a wait until the liquid begins to bubble with significance, cotton wool is placed, with the zeal of the mystic, into the magic liquid, the plastic syringe sighs as the plunger is drawn up, hell will cease now, heaven's dance begins again caressing the verse in the mind of the poet. Those shackles will float away again, the needle fits snugly onto the syringe, the singer of dreams smacks his arm, the tube becomes swollen, and the spike pierces the purple vein, deliverance from the world. As the plunger draws upwards a serpent of blood dances into the cloudy liquid, thank god, a hit the first time, the plunger pushes this chemical dream out of the syringe into his arm, he trembles ahrrrrr.........the warmth radiates up the arm rushing into the catacombs which were his mind.......this heat begins to permeate the entirety of his body, he is blessed into the Kingdom, the stigmata on his arm are aching with knowledge now: peace dawns with lilies floating in a pool of violet.......this is the innocence denied him as a child. A crisp autumn wind caresses brown and blood-red leaves into a frenzy of swirls. The psychiatric hospital sits alone in the platitudes of the rustic. It is a place where light is reciprocated between the damned, on occasion. The outsiders, ostracized by a world

As the plunger draws upwards a serpent of blood dances into the cloudy liquid, thank god, a hit the first time, the plunger pushes this chemical dream out of the syringe into his arm, he trembles ahrrrrr.........the warmth radiates up the arm rushing into the catacombs which were his mind.......this heat begins to permeate the entirety of his body, he is blessed into the Kingdom, the stigmata on his arm are aching with knowledge now: peace dawns with lilies floating in a pool of violet.......this is the innocence denied him as a child. A crisp autumn wind caresses brown and blood-red leaves into a frenzy of swirls. The psychiatric hospital sits alone in the platitudes of the rustic. It is a place where light is reciprocated between the damned, on occasion. The outsiders, ostracized by a world of squares which cannot accept circles, seek sanctuary in this place of shadows, a place of vibrations. The ambulance cruises through a bleak, but welcoming afternoon; he hopes that the hospital will be like a monastery, a convent where the anguished will be saturated with love? What strikes him when the nurses help him undress is the crisp institutional nature of this place. The bed has white sheets, they feel like there've been bleached. The nurses wear uniform, the women are dressed as nurses in a general hospital, the men in identical hospital suits. A doctor, in a white coat, drifts onto the ward; he smiles: 'Nurse will give you an injection. You are safe here. I'll see you soon. Rest the mind and build-up your body.'

'Thank-you. I'm quite interested in Jung's work.'

'We will talk about many things, but rest now.'

Two nurses puzzle towards the poet, lost in a dance of the tragic and ego which pervades these places. They carry a grey cardboard tray, its edges raised to prevent any deviance from the task allotted by the god in a white coat, on it are a plastic syringe, same model as used by the dreamers, a brown glass ampoule which rests in supplication, in this place the drugs are checked before administration, cotton wool and a pink plaster which cannot hide the wounds given in Eden. They smile, he lies with the fear of the finite resounding around this howling labyrinth of unquiet spirits, and the exorcism begins. Words drip like droplets of sweat from their tight mouths:

'Now we can do this the easy way or you can make it difficult.'

The dreamer is metamorphosed into a patient, he lies resistant, but he recognizes in their eyes something of the priest draped in black, preparing to utter words of absolution. The needle is eased into hard muscle, it is painful, a largactal daze strikes his body like the thud of thunder in a prison cell, the mind does not begin to relax, there is nothing vaguely opiate about this chemical, rather it is like being struck by a truncheon, battered by the blows of mediocrity. Twelve hours pass in a void without a flicker of consciousness. He begins to re-surface; the vision is blurred, but intact. At the foot of his bed sit two nurses, his sight focuses on them, but he becomes aware of other beds, two lines of iron bed-frames on which are mattresses with alternate orange and lime green covers. On these ships of dreams, within thehouse of whispers, sit these mystics of the psyche. Ten days on and he is allowed to wander around the ward, the watchful gaze of the uniformed ones observe his tracks of body and mind. The voice of the ward's patriarch booms through the ward:

Medication time, come and get your pills

everyone.'
Those shackles are about to be locked into place again as an orderly queue forms. The poet ponders that this may be a form of victim hood? But who are the victims: patients or nurses? The rigid frame of the clinic's entrance anticipates the medication, it is blocked by a steel trolley, behind which stand two nurses, on its top lie ordered rows of medicine tots awaiting the sticky brown syrup: chlorpromazine. The taste is foul and the odour unpleasant, it slips down the throat like swallowing the sulphur of Hades. However this young man feels an empathy with the flowers of the night, he becomes aware that he has found his home; the asylum. Gradually the poet learns the rules and mores of this place, he grasps the nature of the hierarchies, the maneuvering of staff and patient, the look of fear which registers in the eyes of some when approached by a certain nurse, the life of this organism resounds through his mind, he can resist actively or passively, on occasion to defy the authority of this place, other times to play the role of submission, to appear broken, its all part of living in these places, it's the way you learn to survive. But his mind is never subordinated before their high alters of absurdity with those candles which burn like acid inthe soul. Of course there are caring staff; he learns to seek them out, other outsiders who also seek sanctuary in the hospital, but on the other side of the fence, sometimes the boundaries become rather confused when we live in this place and some of the nurses sing a similar song. It is 1977 and the world still inhales the breath of revolution, we aredizzy with vision, each other and ourselves. However the revolution has its enemies in these places. As evening caresses this tormented place the poet decides that the revolution should be alive in this palace of dreams. He resists with his body, his body is like a weapon which cannot be soothed with the language of oppression. This resistance is the poetry of darkness; it is the drama of the physical, so he begins to refuse food, a week later and he becomes accustomed to the ache of hunger in his stomach, and the verse which is his defiance. The retreat into the damp cell of the body becomes a reason for existence and his sigh to the night has become a song with all the oppressed. The situation begins to tighten like an elastic band which is gradually stretched until its tension winds up to make a doll dance. The nurses are not detached from the drama, they are part of this whole scene, and the atmosphere begins to become heightened as his refusal of food enters its fourth week. The white-coated ones come to check his blood-pressure on the hour and he is transferred to the disturbed unit. Here electricity buzzes every breakfast between the poet and the nurses, they want him to eat the greasy bacon and beans which is shuffled before him. The struggle reaches intensity again at lunch and returns like a ratinvested plague as tea-time approaches, but his poetry still flows with the ink of memory and the frost of autumn in

these places. Venus also lives on the disturbed unit, she is 18, has shoulder length ginger hair, crimson cheeks and a ribbon of freckles across her nose, she wears faded blue denim jeans and an orange tee-shirt. Venus is huddled in a wheel-chair, the poet wonders who she is, is she "cool", perhaps she's a real human-being? Venus and the poet are like flowers in a wasteland of twisted iron. They soon become aware of a reciprocal vibration:

The bastards, I jumped, wanted to fly and die, know what I mean?'

she aches.

'Yes, yes I do, I want to bring this rotten edifice crashing down with

me.

They're the living dead, you know Jesus said: "Let the dead bury

their dead".

My name is Venus; I take acid and speed, do you?'

'Yea I do'.

Venus smiles and says: 'Let's trip in the bin'.

Their conversation is the dialogue of dreams in the dream-factory, the asylum, but these visions can be aborted.

The staff have taken away her wheelchair and hidden it somewhere on the ward. They say she can walk, but Venus's legs are smashed and the nurses know this. They don't like young people with a vision which defies a world which has its stone grinding lives into the flour of platitudes. The nurses are sitting on cheaply upholstered wine-red chairs at random points around a white-washed room. They stare with eyes which burrow into your most hidden being, there is no escape here. One method of control is to take the patients cigarettes and issue them hourly, the hours begin to revolve around the next cigarette, this becomes the accepted form of communication in these places, and all other forms of human contact are frowned upon on this unit. In this place, when you're 17 or 18, resistance becomes the ideology of despair and this gradually becomes the only hope, the dream. It is Sunday and as usual the porters bring the meal trolley. It is a steel box with draws which contains dinner, then beneath pudding; on each corner is a castor with a black rudder tyre. The nurses plug it into a socket, already the tension begins to rise. Venus needs a cigarette, she has to drag herself across the floor to the charge-nurses office, and she understands the process of subordination on this ward:

'Please nurse, may I have a cigarette.'

A snapped reply: 'You know there aren't any.'

We all know that Venus's mum brought in 20 at visiting time the evening before:

Icarus Rising

'Please nurse, a smoke.'

'Clear off.' Is the response.

'I only want a smoke.'

'If you carry on there's an injection, you don't want that, do you?'

Venus pulls her broken body across the carpet; tears are washing the pain from her face, she sobs silently. These places could be like interminable night. The poet sits at a white vinyl covered dinning table, he feels dizzy. A nurse pushes a plate of cabbage, sprouts, roast potatoes, beef and gravy before his trembling face: '

'You will eat today, you will eat this.'

His silence has more resonance than any shout. The ward-sister slams a food liquidizer on the table, it has a brown square base, about 4x4 inches, on top of this is a cone shaped container, his dinner is slopped into this, the lid is snapped into place, a button pushed, there is a whirling noise, the product is thick green liquid, the lid is removed and the contents poured into a beaker:

'You will drink this, now!' '

I'm not drinking that slime.'

Lightning between patient and nurses sizzles and sparks. They surround him, one gives him a poke in the ribs, their loud voices sting his mind; this seems, to him, like a manifestation of Dante's worst dreams. The torment continues, eventually he agrees to drink their potion and swallows the green slime. His stomach contracts and expels the liquid, he spews uncontrollably. Before the poet lies a pool of yellow vomit and green bile. They demand:

'Clean that up immediately.'

This sounds, to the poet, like an expulsion of the Fallen from heaven; he is cast into an abyss of fear where the flames of their anger lick his soul and body in frenzy of domination:

I'm not cleaning that up; you made me drink the stuff.'

He was 17 and the night had become very dark. It will be over a year before he will see the outside of the hospital and the doctors never did discuss Jung with him. The only comfort, for this poet, was to scribe the voices of other outsiders in his verse.

Nigel Pearce

Was that just a...dream?

Rattle-snake in the mind of the passenger of the red-bus, Midland Red bus, rolls past the Red house, where he was sent by the Party, but lost the argument on the nature of the Soviet Union with a solitary, in many ways, shop steward. Peter the steward, who sat like a 'desert-rat' about to chisel away at the statue of Ozymandias behind a poorly vanished square table occasionally taking sips from a single whisky, it would take him exactly an hour to consecrate this small tumbler made of thick glass, then the next. The wizardry of words took place, over many, many evenings, but it was John from the 4th International who had cast the spell, the most potent of all the enchantment of ideas. The passenger sits coiled in faded blue jeans of a generation wandering to ...'try to concentrate that those other people on the bus do exist as matter....' The veil was lifted on another trip which had burnt out his eyes like acid only to reveal other landscapes, looking deeper into fathomless ocean within, hopeless holes of introspection which he fell through. People begin to inhale and exhale, lets breath, gulp in one great gush of oxygen. Did the passenger just say: 'Am I breathing?' No it was that lizard sitting opposite. There are two rows of sets huddled into this rectangle crate called a bus, divided by a two foot gangway which has a matt black covering worn by the interminable daily journeys of these people, back and forth, going and coming. Are they really sitting in a glasshouse and, he thinks, should I throw a couple of stones; But then just mumbles into his hand: 'Wake up your predators, just spit out your poison'. The bus is travelling along a channel, a grove worn by journeys that shudder through the grid of a town and then winds through equally ordered suburban excuses for those who think they belong, but none belong here...Wham! Was that green, not lawn manicured, but grass really unapologetically muddy in winter, fine like a young man's dawn in spring, strong and thick as a women's at the zenith of her lunar arch and stiff with frost at the ache of her going to sleep. I woke up and almost fell out of the door of that can on four rather worn looking tyres while it was cruising away, it wasn't wreaked but then neither was I. Not 'stoned' that is, but dreamy and floating. Had that nightmare ended last night, the last incarnation of a flea? He glanced at the pavement; yes the cracks seem to have attained the status of the chequered symmetry of a chessboard. I drifted away, the cracks had now become caverns in the rumble which I was walking through, above and below simultaneously, a kind of marriage of heaven and hell, most stop reading Blake at the moment. Certainly round the corner of the first detached red-bricked house in this little street is a precipice who begs you to throw yourself over into a ravine of distorted faces whose eyes weep into each other.

'You weirdo', 'Hippie scum' 'Loony commie', you ...'

'What did you say?

'You heard, fresh out of the nut-house again?

The jeers had come from a group of lads who were vaguely approaching puberty and haven't quite managed the transition walking past the entrance of the red-bricked street. I grasp hold of a tablet of stone deep within me upon which is written in indelible ink; 'the proletariat is the agent of social transformation.' But some seem particularly alienated. At this point he thought it best to continue walking without replying to the last line and turned into niche of the petty-bourgeois. Yes he had indeed lived in the asylum, a huge Victorian community of buildings neglected and becoming derelict, as were most of the patients, nurses and doctors. It just induced that kind of nether world, rich with the odour of brimstone.

I opened the wooden-side gate of the house because 'the parents', preferred me to entered as surreptitiously as possible, definitely not at the front door in view of all the neighbours: 'there's the problem son, they say the daughter is not quite right either', Nobody will like it if I am an incarnation of a flea...they get very worked-up about things like that...mind you what doesn't freak them out

'Hello mum, nice to see you'.

'You didn't tell me you were calling, what have you come for?'

'Just came to see you as dad was at work so we could listen to The Emperor, the piano concerto, you know the Beethoven.'

His mother replied:
'Well if it's cultural, you can come in and I'll make some sandwiches and we can listen; it's a wonderful piece of music you know.'

'Thank you mum.' I recalled her telling me as a child that: 'When he played his piano concertos, he played them with such emotion that the pianos collapsed, were smashed.' We were both quite intense people; mum and I.

What follows was certainly a dream experienced by 'the passenger' as a middle-age man years after his parents death. What were the origins of his nightmare? Repressed unconscious desires, suppressed memories of occurrences to awful to recollect or his internalized fears cleverly manipulated by someone who had an agenda. Who knows where the origins of such an awful descent into such uncharted depths could be? The Narrator alone can stand without the lawyers brief or the biologist's microscope or the supposed privileged knowledge of the psycho-analyst. All she or he can do is to relate an experience. Here is 'the passengers' dream. He took his heavy night sedation as normal whilst listening to the news, within in an hour he was deep in a medication induced sleep, he'd been waking early for many years now, ridiculously early since his mother's death. As in many mornings now he woke around 4.00 or 5.00 a.m., he would apply himself to writing or studying; these were his main endeavours. Political and social isolation had lead to little other fruitful activity. On the few occasions on which he regained that allusive state, sleep, upon returning to bed he would fly through a most extraordinary galaxy of dreams or nightmares. Although disturbing, he was grateful for at least a little more physical rest because after many years he had become exhausted. Also they were of huge fascination to him, if not for others. That night he had woken around 5.00 a.m. but had felt pleasantly drowsy and soon returned to bed. This is an account of what he then experienced whilst slumbering, wrote down immediately upon waking and passed this written record to me, the Narrator. This account is transcribed by me for the purposes of this short-story.

'He was travelling on the local bus out of town which passed a pub that was an old haunt of the revolutionary 'Left'. In those days he had lived a nomadic existence, sleeping on people's floors and took large amounts of amphetamine sulphate and L.S.D. but constantly read and wrote both poetry and prose. There were regular admissions into the local psychiatric hospital and he neglected his appearance, but in a certain hippie style. On the bus he felt particularly alienated from the other people and estranged from reality. Upon reaching the village where his parents lived he disembarked from the bus, he wasn't in a drug induced altered state of consciousness but felt separated from reality. When turning into the little street of detached red-bricked houses where his parents lived, he was verbally abused by a group of young men, but made a verbal repost. As normal he knocked on the side door of the house because of his parent's position regarding the neighbours. His mother opened the door and eventually made him some sandwiches and they agreed to listen to their favourite composer; Beethoven. Mum sat on a three person settee and he on the matching armchair. The black vinyl disc of an old EMI recording of Beeethoven dad did not allow the playing of classical music while he was in house. The 'familiar', a black cat of

Icarus Rising

someone known to them appeared on the carpet. His mother began to shrink and metamorphosed into a hideous reptile, but as this occurred she emitted a speck of dust which floated around the room. The cat began to swipe its paws towards the floating speck. His mother shouted: 'If the cat gets that speck I'm done for.' The cat had caught the speck with its paws and was pulling it towards its whiskers, his mother was disappearing rapidly. As it was inhaling the speck he didn't know what to do, an atheist Marxist, he found this all very bizarre, but had previously considered the Roman Catholic priesthood. Not knowing how else to save his mother he dropped to his knees at the side of the sofa bent his head with his long hair in disarray and prayed to the 'Holy Spirit'. The cat disappeared and his mother returned to her normal state. He walked to the record player and removed the disc, splitting it into two as a Catholic priest would the Host at Mass; he then broke off a fragment in the same way a priest does before placing it into a chalice containing the wine. His mother took this and said: 'This will come in handy for our ceremonies.'

He woke and recorded an account in his poetry note book, this is simply a transcription of the dream with no commentary by the Narrator or analysis by the dreamer, but as he recollected it upon regaining consciousness. As it is written.

The passenger wondered, as the bus, the red bus swayed and muttered back to the dome, if on their grid the electricians made any brain cells that weren't fused: 'Cool that our 'scene' is not connected to their grid, hope the 'The Man' is about 'cause I'm waiting for him. Need 'gear' and a nice new set of 'works'. That was really heavy, know what I mean?'

Nigel Pearce

George Orwell's '1984': revisited.

Winston Smith and Julia had been banished by Big Brother to a sandy and wind swept wilderness. Here their flesh was burnt by the relentless sun and their hunger only assuaged by a love which transcended the abysmal curse of the 'Thought-Police'. Bodies almost too raw to touch, they made love with a deep and dark energy which came from a liberated libidinal drive. They had penetrated deep into the Id and like a hurricane that came from their essences banished all banality, intoxicating with interacting unconsciousness'. Other exiles had struggled and heaved their way across the shifting d climbed into incrustations which provided temporary shelter from the blazing sun. These exiles had been drawn from the various strata of the 'Outer Party'. Some accused of tarnishing the purity of 'Newspeak'. Others cast-out for sexual activity which was banned for them and, yet, others for keeping clandestine journals. Big Brother had cast these outsiders into this harsh terrain from where there was no apparent return only after they had been 'de-cultured' and professed their love for Big Bother. Torture had been used until they 'confessed' to their crimes; Electro Convulsive Therapy had been employed as one method to extract these so-called revelations. Then processed in the 'Ministry of Love' they had been accessed as being rehabilitated and therefore needed no further treatment and where cast, apparently broken, into the wilderness. Gradually they had melted into the night like roaming pariahs, but they left sighs like all scavengers and they began to locate each other and form into little bands, almost packs. These groups moved in an every reducing circle until they began to coalesce. When this jell had formed it was inevitable that Winston and Julia would become a beacon, because of their intellectual and erotic challenge to Big Brother and his apparatus the 'Thought Police'. They would guide their comrades through the bitter nights of wilderness and isolation. But passivity began to pervade the group, choking it like a hang-man's noose. Winston and Julia left the group saying:

'We may be gone a little while, its important ideological work, remember love and solidarity.'

They wandered into the wilderness guided by the anti-Father, the antithesis of Big Brother who was the collective memory of Goldstein. They were drawn to a ragged cliff and climbed until exhausted they had reached a crevice hidden by brush. Within lay pure white tablets of stone about the size of a volume of Marx/Engels 'Selected Works', delving into the aperture they found three, a trinity. On their return other members of the group or as they were now calling themselves: 'Revolutionary Proletarian Cell', for

Winston had said long ago: 'If there is hope it lies in the proles.' Upon these stones Winston and Julia, employing the instruments devised by their brothers and sisters, their comrades, began to give tangible form to their abstract thoughts and their physical experiences.

It read, indeed proclaimed: '1) Only the proletariat can overthrow the Party and Big Brother. This is the product of our objective analysis and is our goal 2) We do not know what the subjective conditions are within the proletarian zones, by that we mean there is no awareness of the consciousness of the proletariat; their class consciousness. 3) Consequently the 'Cell' must adopt the tactic of zones of the lost, who by their own activity shall, be found as a class. 4) Any means necessary is, ultimately, justified by the achievement of the ends.' After a number of forages across the wasteland to the workers ghettos, they obtained essential items such as worker's clothes. Gradually they accumulated a collection of items, bits and pieces and like a circling eagle reconnoitred the terrain before swooping on its prey, but the masses weren't the prey , they were the instrument to be employed against the prey. Like the dawn wipes the tyranny of night from the world the 'Cell' began what they believed and had interpreted from Engels as their: 'World historic mission.' As twilight began to dissolve the colours of day they penetrated the worker's zone; then were confronted with an ink black smog which was almost Dickensian and the neglected tower-blocks where the masses existed with the horrors of a life separated from its meaning, its essence, but the 'Cell' would help create this essence even if it required destroying the existential to allow the essence to have a vehicle to articulate itself, allowing the masses to emancipate themselves. Winston and Julia now rested from the 'Cell's period of wandering, assumed the everyday running of their group. Everywhere the belching of factories and the preparations for yet more wars in which the workers would be sacrificed to the insane logic of Big Brother created a terrain of ideological anaemia as well as poverty. The people seemed to walk bent over under the yoke of alienation and be shackled to the hopeless grind of their lives. their intellectual and cultural diet, force-feed, was a combination of sentimentality and pornography which, in totality, had lead to a soporific and subservient proletariat. Winston was despondent: 'How can we organize or ignite these people it's like the task of Sisyphus. All is lost.' Julia replied: 'Let us travel beyond appearance into essence, we may be surprised what we discover find.' constant stream of platitudes and patriotism. Eventually they entered the central areas; here there were just shacks, dismal hovels. Julia suddenly smiled and said: 'It is here that the wound is at its most rancid. It is here where the depths of the oppressed are to be found.'

With a trembling sense of trepidation and expectation Julia and Winston approached one of hovels. They knocked on the flimsy but heavily chained door. A head, well a skull with deep blackened sockets peered around the edge:

'What yer want...best smack we got, ten quid a bag ... blow yer away.'

Julia answered in the language she had learnt in an 'Outer Party' manual of 'prolespeak.

"Cool, we can score here.' 'Yea baby...got any works.'

An emaciated figure unshackled the door and said: 'Best shooting gallery in town man.' Winston and Julia entered this palace of despair, quivering. A man, the 'Man', sat in a haze of tangerine; his eyes seemed like amber jewels glaring like furnaces in the gloom of the shooting gallery. He hovered out of the door leaving the two revolutionaries and the skeletal worker. He groaned: 'Do you up for that other ten quid bag. Just do my business first.' Julia and Winston looked in horror as he slithered up his shirt-sleeve, arms covered in needle marks, bruises and seeping abscesses. He searched pathetically for a vein that wasn't just an inflamed track: 'Got a hit...far out man... ahhrrr cool stuff.' The junkie was how in a haze and flushing blood and water in and out of his syringe, sucking constant stream of platitudes.

Immediately with the force of a passion released from the unconscious by a lover Julia and Winston became aware that this polluted blood with its dream serum was the agent of social transformation. The 'Cell' gathered in the depths of the inner zones and a new line was, this time, enforced by the revolutionary couple on their comrades: 'We had believed that only through the rise in class consciousness and a consequent proletarian revolution could Big Brother, or to be more accurate comrades Big Daddy, can be removed. However it has become apparent it is only through the dissemination of decadence and hedonism particularly through i.v. drug use that the system can be undermined, if not overthrown. This pollution must happen from the base to the pinnacle...only in this way can the next generation be cleansed and emancipated. You remember the ends justify the means by any necessary praxis.' Julia continued: 'Hence decadence contains in itself the apotheosis of the masses.' Winston concluded: 'It is necessary to spread an immorality, almost a plague, it will eventually consume the Party in its entirety and Big Brother Himself. And from these ruins will raise proto-communism.' During the next day/nights the 'Cell' fuelled by what was becoming a contorted, almost distorted, zeal, they spread hard drugs and whatever other encouragement was necessary to propagate the new line. Making money and then investing, reinvesting; wasn't this a little like the cycle of Capital accumulation discovered by Marx? However workers became too ill to work regularly and the Gross Domestic Product began to fall, the destruction of the masses was being used for the emancipation of the masses: to destroy 'double-think', well that's what the 'Cell' had come to believe. They had been in the wilderness so long they had lost touch of their own philosophical concepts; these had become hopeless abstractions without a base in the material, in reality, in the masses. But Big Brother's war-drive finally collapsed and with it the dynamic of His system. Intravenous heroin use became endemic within the 'Inner Party' which was already disintegrating because of factional struggles. Suddenly with the combination of economic failure and a structural crisis in the leadership in the ruling class the 'Cell' (they hadn't made any attempt to recruit members to their group) saw their strategy had proven successful. The problem was though they had destroyed the structure of the system they had also weakened the only force that could replace it; the proletariat. Mistakenly they had believed that an almost sacrificial plague, the immolation of and by the masses through the spreading of dissolute habits and practices was the solution, but it was not.

One morning Julia and Winston stumbled upon a building where the 'tele-screen' was still working, but only just...it was a grey blurred haze with a figure that seemed spectral. They realized it was a dim image of Big Brother. He said solemnly and in a measured tone: 'This is the final analysis. We have reached Omega, therefore the Inner Party has dissolved itself. History and hence Reason or sanity has been concluded. The only option for me is...' He slowly eased a revolver from the desk he was sitting behind: 'Too create my own myth.' He placed the revolved in his month and the 'tele-screen' pang into darkness. As the next few years past a semblance of order returned to society. Methods for treating the previous socio-cultural problems were successfully created and implemented. Julia mused: 'Could Humanity really taste it's essence in these conditions, isn't the freedom for self-destruction a much deeper drive than socio-economic drives.' She realized Big Brother, Big Daddy was just an image from her unconscious, and she had destroyed the symbol of the father from whom she never received love. She grasped a kitchen-knife and in a deliberate and potent act stabbed herself in the heart. But rumours were now beginning to spread. Had Big Brother really committed suicide for the 'tele-screen' had blanked out at the vital moment? Had Big Brother really fled with some close 'Inner Party' comrades into the wilderness as Winston and Julia had years before? Did all this really happen or was it a ghastly delusion projected by some expelled members of the 'Inner Party' which had lead to Julia's suicide? Only you can decide.

Nigel Pearce

On other writers.
Heinrich Heine: poet and revolutionary.

'Ask me not what I have, but what I am.' – Heinrich Heine.
Heinrich Heine was born 1797 in Germany. He was both an important poet in the German 'Romantic' tradition and a revolutionary socialist. These two combine to make Heine pertinent today and a significant figure in proletarian literature. Why? The answer is to be located in the complex interactions between socio-economic forces in the context of History', we may define this as 'Historical Materialism', and the role of the poet in 'alienating' bourgeois conditions i.e. in the relations of Capitalism. Firstly this analysis will briefly define the methodology described as Historical Materialism which is then applied to the crucial question of the 'alienated'Romantic poet'. Four main areas of inquiry will be examined in that context: a) biographical details and Heine's textual material b) the place of Heine in the context of the friendship with Marx and Engels, c) the significance of his role as a poet in the revolutionary movement, d) and finally draw the lessons for the oppressed today we can draw from Heine. Therefore I will illustrate the methodological orientation for this study which is 'Historical Materialism'.
Basically there are two essential philosophical categories which have, indeed, sub-sections. They are 'Idealism' and Materialism': 'The great basic question of all philosophy is that concerning the relation of thinking there are Idealism and Materialism:

'The great basic question of all philosophy is that concerning the relation of thinking and being...which the philosophers have split into two great camps...the camp of Idealism and the various schools of Materialism.

- Engels: 'Ludwig Feuerbach.'
I would like to stress here that the terms 'Idealism' and 'Materialism' are here employed in a specific usage is which described by Maurice Cornforth:

'1) Idealism asserts that the material world is dependent on the spiritual.

2) Idealism asserts that that spirit, or mind, or idea, can and do exist in separation from matter.

3) Idealism asserts that there exists a realm of the mysterious and unknowable, 'above', or 'beyond' or 'behind' what can be ascertained and known by perception, experience and science.' -

- Maurice Cornforth:
'Materialism and the Dialectical Method''

This is not just an abstract debate but is one that has a direct consequence on the future of humanity because mistakes in theory lead to errors on practice and if the 'Universal Class', the proletariat and their vanguard party make them the repercussions are immense. If we choose an incorrect methodology, a wrong way of looking and understanding the world we cannot make the correct 'concrete analysis of concrete situations' (Lenin). So what is 'Materialism': firstly it is the instrument which the working class and its Party arm themselves in the class struggle. Philosophy is partisan; you are either a reactionary or a revolutionary, you are either for the crumbling social order or against it as Marx noted: 'All History is the history of class struggle' and as Trotsky reflected: 'Capitalism has entered its death agony'. Secondly as is apparent in the contrast to 'Idealism' the Materialist schools see 'change' for as Engels noted 'reality is matter in motion. More that that the materialists believe the world is knowable to the masses not just the privileged elite of priests and mystics. So when you apply materialism to History the school of thought to embrace is Historical Materialism, the theory of the oppressed, indeed the hope for humanity, but which is founded in material reality. Lenin encapsulates the whole conception with insight and theoretical penetration:

'The history of philosophy has shown clearly that Marxism contains nothing of the least resemblance to 'sectarianism' in the sense of any closed up, fossilized doctrine...On the contrary.The whole genus of Marx consists in his giving answers to questions which the progressive thinking of humanity had already posed.'

- Lenin: 'The Three Sources and Component Parts of Marxism'. Having established the method used in this paper it isHaving established the method used in this paper it is necessary to examine the role of the poet, the estranged poet. Trotsky had commented that poets have to
: '...reshape the world of feelings. Not everybody is
capable of that.'-Trotsky: 'Literature and Revolution.
Heine also commented on the poet in bourgeois society:

'Since the heart of the poet is the central point of the world it must at present times be woefully torn. Those who are able to boost that their hearts have remained whole are only admitting that they have a prosaic narrow heart'.

- Heine.

Heine was a poet in the tradition of German romanticism which was initially a feudal reaction to the French revolution and the English industrial revolution and it flourished during the reaction of its collapse. But some had supported the French Revolution and were profoundly disappointed by its failure. Hence among this group of poets and intellectuals appeared a revolutionary dimension to German Romanticism that began to rise of which Heine was a part. Therefore, but avoiding idealist analysis, we can understand how poets such as Heine embraced the cause of the oppressed and marginalized. Heine's life and work can be seen clearly in the tradition of a combination of the 'new' with a love of popular culture and folk-lore. Of course the 'new' at the time included mould breaking composers such as Ludwig Beethoven who has now been appropriated by elements within the Establishment. The 'novel' was developing into a revolutionary art form challenging the courtly literature of medieval time. The young Heinewas caught up in this cauldron. However two unrequited loves who haunted him throughout his life, both were cousins: Amalie and Therese. In poems such as: 'allnachtlich im traume' he expresses the intensity of his emotions: raw and spontaneous.Here is the first verse translated into a popular version by the Marxist Hal Draper:

'Nightly I hear you in dreams – you speak With kindness sincerest I throw myself, weeping aloud and weak At your sweet feet, my dearest.'

- Heine.

Many have known these emotions, indeed some the acts themselves when intoxicated by love. This was published in a collection called: 'Book of Songs' in 1827. Around this time, perhaps heart-broken, and certainly by politically motivation an atmosphere of cynicism combined by a mockery of authority becomes apparent and will continue in much of his

socialist tone with poems such as The Weavers Song' which was about an insurrection of weavers in 1844:

'From darkened eyes no tears are falling

With gritted teeth we sit here calling Germany, listen, ere we disperse, We weave your shroud with a triple curse We weave we are weaving.

- Heine.

This was written in the same year as Marx wrote his great study of 'alienation' and 'struggle': Economic and Philosophical Manuscripts'. Heine also caught the revolutionary consciousness inherent in the proletariat. As with all utopian socialists, which often draw on a 'primitive Christianity' Heine didn't understand the inevitable consequence of the rise of capitalism was a working class revolution which would create more for the majority in a higher synthesis both materially and culturally. Rather he tended to see socialism as a kind of sensual monastic community. Nevertheless Marx was an admirer of Heinz's work and maintained a close friendship as his daughter Eleanor Marx wrote:

'He loved him just as much as his works, and was as

indulgent as can be towards his political weaknesses. Poets, he declared, are peculiar people. You cannot measure them with the usual scale for normal people'.

- Eleanor Marx: Neue Zei

Heine's poem 'Germany: A Winter's Tale' provides us with a vision of the future:

'A new song, a better song, oh friends I'll sing for you. Here on earth we mean to make our paradise comes true. We mean to be happy here on earth.

- Heine.

Heinrich Heine was both a great Romantic poet and a revolutionary writer. His flaw was an inability to differentiate the utopian from the authentic revolutionary traditions, a poet of his times and still an inspiration to the oppressed today.

Nigel Pearce

Existentialism and the role of the poet today.

"Vertigo is anguish to the extent that I am afraid
not of falling over the precipice, but of throwing
myself over."
- Jean-Paul Sartre.

Existentialism, unlike other philosophical systems, stresses the
subjective experience of human beings in our daily lives. An early
reference to this problem of everyday life is in Blase Pascals's:
Pensees. He argued that without a God our lives would be absurd
and sad, people would create goals and "work", but all these
endeavours would be meaningless. To escape this situation Pascal
rejected atheism. Kierkegaard and Nietzsche can be seen as the
founders of the Existentialist movement, although they didn't use the
term to describe themselves. Both lived in the 19th century and,
following Pascals work, were interested in the problems of
meaninglessness. However, they went beyond Pascals and asserted
a new freedom for human beings:

"truth is subjectivity."
- Kierkegaard.

This means that the most important thing for a human being is the
inner relationship we have with existence: an inner relationship with
"absurdity."
Nietzsche proclaimed

"the death of God."
- Nietzsche.

His words would shake and transform the experience of Western
civilisation from the late 19th century onwards. When D.H.Lawrence
read Nietzsche he said:

"If there is nothing to believe in, we must, therefore,
undermine everything."
- D.H.Lawrence.

We can see the themes of both Kierkegaard and Nietzsche running
through 20th century Existentialism.

However, I would like briefly to examine the literary existentialists
and the rise
of a concomitant dissident sub-culture. The experience of
"absurdity" and feelings of guilt without a source are explored in the
literature of Franz Kafka. His characters are accused of crimes they
have no knowledge of by anonymous authorities, a kind of nightmare
of patriarchal societies without a concept of forgiveness.
Dostoevsky's novel 'Crime and Punishment' is about those who
commit apparently irrational acts and live on the margins of society,

those who are cast out of the social system: the outsiders. In the 1950's and 1960's existentialist writing again became the literature of authenticity and was articulating a sub-culture which rejected the artistic forms and values of commodity capitalism. The poetry of Allen Ginsberg and the surrealistic novels of William Burroughs became known as 'Beat' writing. It embraced the spontaneity of the black jazz musicians that they admired. Their emphasis on "authenticity" was inspired by existentialism and they became a significant cultural force. 'Beat' culture was bohemian in nature and advocated disengaging with "straight" or mainstream society and living in a dissident sub-culture. In the 1960's and 1970's a "counter-culture" of people inspired by the writing and life-style of the 'Beats', by Timothy Leary advocating the use of L.S.D. as a means of attaining a chemical "Enlightenment", the rise of revolutionary social movements and Jean-Paul Sartre's existentialist philosophy becoming widely read all combined to create a crisis in international capitalism and its agents of social control such as patriarchal authority and the nuclear family. The shackles on our consciousness were being cast off and the "wage-slavery" (Marx) of late-capitalism was being challenged by those who were disaffected and by the
. revolutionary sections of the proletariat
I would now like to explore Jean-Paul Sartre's existentialism in a little more detail. A core concept is that "Existence precedes essence."
- Jean- Paul Sartre.
As there is not a primal source to create a human essence, because "God is dead.", then human beings are confronted by the question:"what is the nature of my existence?" For Sartre we create our own "essence" or "being": "Human reality can receive its ends
neither from outside or from so called
inner nature."
- Jean- Paul Sartre.
We, therefore, create are own identities which are the source of existential freedom, but this causes anxiety in an absurd world:
"it is anguish that wo/man gets from
the consciousness of freedom."
- Jean-Paul Sartre.
But this "freedom" and the "anguish" it provokes can be overwhelming and we can retreat into what Sartre called "Bad Faith".
"we flee anguish by attempting to
apprehend ourselves from without
as an "Other" or as a thing."
- Jean-Paul Sartre.
This "Other" can be the people we meet or, as Simone de Beauvoir argued in her study 'The Second Sex', that in patriarchal social

systems women are perceived as the "Other" of the male subject. What is the role of the poet and artist today? We should write about the "absurd" and relate to those who live on the periphery of society. The writer, to quote Sartre must always engage "on the side of freedom". He developed this idea in 'What is Literature' by arguing that committed literature must always create imagined worlds against the exploitation of 'late-capitalism' and, therefore, confront all forms of oppression e.g. homophobia and racism. The freedom that the writer has is itself constrained by the boundaries of any given epoch because art, like any other ideological manifestation, is the product of complex socio-economic and political relationships. Sartre was to argue that existentialism itself was only "an ideological moment" within Marxism and that

"Marxism is the one philosophy of our
time which we cannot go beyond."

- Jean -Paul
Sartre

Again poets, artists and their supporters are in the vanguard of the global struggle against bourgeois hegemony and its agents. Our task is clear...

"...we must reconquer humanity
with Marxism."

- Jean-Paul Sartre.

Icarus Rising

On Elise Cowen (1933-1962): woman 'Beat' poet.

"In the 1950's if you were male you could be a rebel,
But if you were female your family had you locked-
up. There were women, I knew them, their families
put them in institutions, they were given electric
shocks treatments".

- Scobie (1994).

During the 1950's in America a literary bohemianism developed
which was similar to the decadence of late 19th century Paris,
indeed the poetry of Charles Baudelaire and his essays on hashish
helped form the psyche of the sub-culture which became known as
'Beat'.'

Hashish, like all other solitary delights, makes the
individual useless to society, and also makes society unnecessary to
the individual.

' - Baudelaire (1966) p39.

These writers and dreamers, rejected the mass consumerism of post
war American society which was itself fuelled by arms spending (see
Kidron (1968) for a Marxist analysis of how capitalism is temporary
stabilized, economically, by arms spending) and embraced the 'new'
in both art and life-style. They seperated themselves from
mainstream or "straight" culture which they saw as bourgeois and
corrupt with its "nice" families and "nice" people who were simply
ideological replicas of the ruling class and its shallow culture. Indeed
these "nice" people had bought the world to the brink of nuclear
annihilation with a combination of U.S. imperialism and the
consequences of the "degeneration" of the revolution in the Soviet
Union. The 'Beats' also rebelled against the stagnant literary forms
and themes which had ossified western culture in the post-war
period. William Burroughs used novels e.g. 'Naked Lunch' and Allen
Ginsberg transformed the world of poetry with his poem 'Howl' in
1956.They wrote about people who live on the existential edge,
those who Jean-Paul Sartre said lived "authentically". Indeed
Ginsberg's 'Howl' was inspired by Carl Solomon whom he had met in
Bellevue mental hospital. In the spring of 1953 Ginsberg and a
young woman named Elise Cowen went out together on a "date".
Elise had been born into a wealthy but unstable family:

Mr Cowen was given to threats and rages; Mrs
Cowen to recriminations and tears'.

- Johnson (1993)

As Elise had grown up she'd developed an aversion to "straight"
society, locking herself in her room and reading Ezra Pound and
Dylan Thomas. She began to neglect her appearance, but still went

to university. Elise didn't succeed academically at college; but this was because she had an independent mind and spirit which wasn't subordinated to the dictates of her professors. Her state of mind began to deteriorate further at this time as she began to regularly use mind altering drugs, her poetry brilliantly sketches the demise into depression and later into psychosis:

Death...
Death I'm coming Wait for me I know you're be at
the subway station'
Here it is possible to be aware of Elise's knowledge of one of her favourite poets, Ezra Pound:
In a station at the Metro
'The apparition of these faces in a crowd
; Petals on a wet, black bough'.
- Pound (1975 p53).

Here both Pound and Cowen convey a sense of isolation and alienation from mass society. Elise makes an (at the time) revolutionary comment on marriage:

Or wait till rot down
With the majestic orange
She stuck on her finger
- Cowen (1996) p162.

Elise has expressed the absurdity of the 1950's American culture with a beautiful eloquence which is gained from having experienced the depths of depression and the 'highs' of amphetamine abuse. Her poetic technique breaks down the traditional form of earlier writers and the fragmentation of lines is suggestive of both a literary experimentation and a dislocated awareness, but most importantly it is an authentic consciousness in the face of death, which with the possibility of a nuclear war, the shadow which hung over the 'Beat' writers. Elise fell in love with Allen Ginsberg and thought they were "twin souls". In the same way as many people with mental illness do she perceived connections and associations which most people would not. Elise believed that because she and Ginsberg had both been patients, at different times, in Bellevue psychiatric hospital this was a 'sign' they should become lovers. They and their friends were mostly poets centralized round Colombia University, but they overlapped with some older writers, such as William Burroughs, with whom they would form the core of the Beat movement. They had a relationship, but Allen Ginsberg "came out" as being gay and moved in with Peter Orlovsky. He would always refer to Elise as "the intellectual madwoman". Her friend commented:

Icarus Rising

'Elise was a moment in Allen's life.
In Elise's life Allen was an eternity'.
- Joyce Johnson (1983)

She began a love affair with a woman called Shelia, but this was a
failure and other attempts to find the love she hadn't found in her
family also proved to be fruitless. Elise was sometimes hospitalized,
but she would seem more dispirited as a result. Her drug use
increased at this time with the stimulants being used in conjunction
with hallucinogenic drugs. The, almost, obsession of the 'Beat' poets
with drugs and death can also be located in other revolutionary
literary movements. located in other revolutionary literary
movements. An example of this is Romanticism [see Hayter (1968)].
Samuel Taylor Coleridge was a leading member of this movement,
who wrote one of his most significant poems, 'Kubla Khan', under
the influence of opium:

> Xanadu did Kubla Khan' A stately pleasure dome
> decree: Where Alpha, the sacred river, ran
> Through caverns measureless to man Down to a
> sunless sea'
> - Coleridge (1996)

p 229.
Coleridge's companion Thomas De Quincey claimed opium allowed
him to:

> 'By signs in heaven-by changes on earth-by
> pulses in secret rivers...and hieroglyphs
> written on the tablet e brain...to gain the
> words'. - De Quincey (1999) p 17.

Did I go mad... '
Did I go mad in my mother's womb
Waiting to get out ...
On my brain are welts from the moving that never moves
On my brain are the welts from the endless stillness'
Here Elise describes the sometimes almost physical experience of
mental illness, but also a sense of the descant into eternal void.
Some within the 'Beat' movement were interested in a form of 'hip'
Buddhism with the mystical states of nothingness being augmented
by peyote.
'I don't want to intone "See how she suffers" "See how she suffers"
(The sting of eyes reminds) That not really, or only I mean-among
other things I am not
permitted to feel that much tick tock'
'But that the truth I guess of (Even were I to KNOW it) Is

EVERYONE'S And what is not this, is a rag flapping
sometimes on the window in the wall across the shaft
Just more waiting, with bells on, And the Truth, is it only the
FACT of WAITING,
the flash at the end of cosmic striptease?
I wants a little something for itself Unique,
a single word treasure act perfection If only to give away
Only to "He scatters his blood on the street
Love? Is this where, what, why Love, loving-all this time?'
                                        - Cowen (1996) p 163.
By 1962 Elise had become very ill with hepatitis and psychosis and
was admitted into Bellevue Hospital, she was discharged against
doctor's advice into a private hospital. Whilst a patient there Elise's
friend Leo Skir visited and later published parts of the conversation:

'She looked fine, better than I'd ever seen her, neat, clean. But she
was mad, quite mad. She felt the City (New York City) had machines
trained on all her thoughts and also that she could here them, the
New York City workers, foolish, bored, boring, mean-souled people.
She described to me in detail the four people, two men, two women
assigned to her. '

        Elise, I said, 'you're paranoid.' 'No,' she said,
        'I'm not'
              . - Skir (1970).
She was discharged into the 'care' of her parents, they confined her
and Elise jumped through a closed window to her death. Cruelly her
parents destroyed Elise's poetry after her death; but fortunately her
friends had kept some copies. In the study 'Minor Characters' Joyce
Johnston makes an incisive comment on Elise's life:
        'She (Elise) could never put on a mask.
           ' - Johnson (1983).
Elise was never published in her life-time, but is now regarded as an
important Beat poet.

Bibliography.

Baudelaire, Charles (1999) [1966] Les Paradis artificiels in Writing on Drugs. London: Routledge.

Coleridge, Samuel Taylor (1996) [1797] in Samuel Taylor Coleridge: Selected Poems. London: Penguin Books.

Cowen, Elise (1996) in Women of the Beat Generation. Berkeley: Conari Press.

De Quincey, Thomas (1999) [1822] Confessions of an English Opium-Eater in Writing on drugs. London: Routledge.

Hayter, Alethea (1968). Opium and the Romantic Imagination. London: Faber and

Faber. Johnson, Joyce (1983) Minor Characters. London: Methuen

Kidron, Mike (1968) Western Capitalism since the War. London.

Pound, Ezra (1975) Selected Poems 1908-1969.London: Faber and Faber.

Scobie (1974) from Stephen Scobie's account of the Naropa Institute tribute to Ginsberg, July 1974. Skir, Leo (1970) Elise Cowen: A brief Memoir of the Fifties in Evergreen Review.

Nigel Pearce

Kate Chopin and her novella: 'The Awakening'

"The consequences of realization are
suicide or recovery".
- Albert Camus (1942).

This analysis will examine the drowning of Edna Pontellier in Kate Chopin's novella 'The Awaking'. Her suicide can only be understood in the general context of the text. This text and her death will be analysed in the context of three competing models: Marxism, existentialism and Radical Feminism. The Marxist perspective will argue that Edna's death is the consequence of the oppression experienced within the family unit when it is unresolved by social revolution and the collectivisation of family life. An existentialist perspective, alternatively, understands her death as the product of an existential crisis and a rational response to the "absurdity" of the human condition. Finally, I shall examine some Radical Feminist analysis of Edna's death which conceptualizes her suicide as a response to patriarchal gender relationships and as an embracing of Matriarchy.

From a Marxist understanding the bourgeois family, in which Edna lives, is seen as the matrix of women's oppression. It is theorized as an institution which grew out of the development of private property and its transmission through the male line. The formation of the family unit is represented as the:

"world historic defeat for the female sex".
- Engels (1884).

Her husband is the epitome of the bourgeois man:

"He looks at his wife as one looks at a
piece of private property".
- Chopin (1889).

This is an illustration of women's subjection in the modern family which is exacerbated under capitalism because social relations are "commoditised" i.e. as a result of alienation from our "species being" (Marx) or essence people perceive each other as an "alien object" (Marx"), as an "exchange value" (Marx) in the market place.

Edna lives in the bourgeoisie; this is stifling her awaking, the comprehension of her self. She is surrounded by an oppressive culture:

"The mother-woman seemed to prevail that
summer at Grand Isle.............They were
women who worshipped their husbands".
- Chopin (1889).

But to her credit, in the context of this analysis, Edna is "not a mother-woman":

"this made Edna Pontellier different from

125

the crowd".

- Chopin (1889).

Although estranged from her class, the bourgeoisie, she is not a part of the proletariat, who are, by the nature of their relationship to the "means of production" (Marx) the agents of revolutionary transformation. Edna walks into the sea:

"Looked into the distance.......then sunk again".

- Chopin (1889).

Edna had vision, she "looked", which is the potential for emancipation. But because she does not have an "objective" role to play in the social transformation of capitalism i.e. in proletarian revolution, she can only be seen as a victim of the bourgeois family and her class. Edna, therefore, like her socio-economic class drowns in the sea of History. Her suicide can be seen as a metaphor for the failure of the bourgeoisie and its institutions to resolve the contradictions of capitalism.

For the existentialists the most significant aspect of modernity is that which was proclaimed by Nietzsche:

"The greatest of recent events is that God is dead".

- Nietzsche (1882).

If there is not a Divine Being it follows there is not a primal source for reality, without a primal source there cannot be a preordained essence for reality, hence "existence precedes essence" (Jean-Paul Sartre). Therefore we, firstly, existentialists would argue, live in an" absurd" world without meaning, but, secondly, we exist to create our own meaning or essence. This is the "freedom" which is the burden of modern humanity, we create ourselves. Camus argues that in the world:

"man feels himself an alien, a stranger. His exile
is without remedy".

- Camus (1942).

However, this knowledge only comes with "realization". This "realization" or "awakening" begins to take place in Edna:

"She was making the acquaintance of new conditions
in herself.............she did not yet suspect".

- Chopin (1889).

In 'The Myth of Sisyphus' Camus addresses, what he considers, to be the ramifications of the "absurdity" of the human condition in relation to the existential "freedom" described above in the context of a person living "authentically" i.e. with an awareness of, what the existentialists regard as "nothingness", the void left by "the death of God". He ponders this and concludes that there is:

"only one truly serious philosophical problem, that is
suicide".

- Camus (1942).

The figure of Sisyphus, drawn from Greek mythology, is punished by the gods for having attempted to defy death. His punishment is to push a stone up a hill, which then rolls down and repeat this process eternally. Here Camus provides his unique contribution to existentialist philosophy, human life is not only "absurd", but it is harsh. However, even in this situation there is hope, he argues, for humanity, because the 'Absurd' itself becomes the creator which animates the artist or poet:

"If the world was clear, art would not exist".

- Camus (1942).

Edna experiences an artistic awaking while listening to Mademoiselle Reisz playing a Chopin Impromptu; she begins to weep and asserts:

"I am becoming an artist".

- Chopin (1889).

So, Edna has experienced an "existential awaking" and an artistic epiphany and says:

"It is better to wake up......to suffer, rather
than remain a dope to illusions all one's life".

- ibid.

The consequences of her awaking will be suicide rather than recovery. She walks on the deserted beach, Chopin uses Pathetic Fallacy:

"A bird with a broken wing was beating the air
above, reeling, fluttering, circling down disabled,
down to the water".

- ibid.

This is extremely potent imagery for Edna has flown from the cage of bourgeois convention, but now after her awaking, her rebellion, the embracing of an "authenticity" she has crushed to the ground. Edna casts off her clothes:

"For the first time in her life she stood naked
in the air.She felt like some new born creature".

- ibid.

She stands naked physically, but also with her whole being casting off what an existentialist would call "bad faith" (Sartre) i.e. the illusions of conventional life, she is living on the existential edge. In Sartre's existentialist novel 'Nausea' the character Antoine Roquentin is in a similar position:

"The thing (existence...flows through me.
I'm filled with it. It's nothing: I am the Thing.
Existence, liberated, detached, it floods over
me".

- Sartre (1938).

Hence from an existentialist perspective Edna's drowning can be seen as positive, an embracing of "good faith" (Sartre). This position is rewarding, but fails to understand the role of the structure of families and socio-economic class in her death.

For some feminist theorists Edna's death is also viewed positively. Sandra Gilbert argues "she dies and is then resurrected as Venus, swimming into a female paradise and out of Flaubertian "realism" into a new kind of myth/metaphysical fantasy". Another feminist critic, Elizabeth LeBlanc suggests that Edna and the ocean "join in the ultimate lesbian moment". From a patriarchal theory feminist perspective these positive interpretations of Edna's suicide are persuasive and I have sympathy with them. However, they both fail to appreciate the role of the bourgeois family unit as the basis of women's oppression and, therefore, of Edna's suicide. They also avoid the significant role of socio-economic class. Ultimately, I would argue, Edna's death was the product of the absence of a proletarian revolution with the subsequent failure to create communism with its abolition of private property, which following Engels' position, would lead to the end of the family unit and, hence, the end of the oppression of women.

Nigel Pearce

Bibliography.

Camus, A. (1942) The Myth of Sisyphus, Harmondsworth: Penguin Books.

Chopin, K. (1889) The Awakening, Chicago & New York: Stone & Company.

Engels, F. (1884) The Origins of the Family, Private Property and the State, London: Lawrence and Wishart.

Gilbert, S. (1983) The Second Coming of Aphrodite: Kate Chopin's Fantasy
of Desire, U.S.A: Kenyon Review.

LeBanc, E. (1996) The Metaphorical Lesbian: Edna Pontellier, U.S.A.:Tulsa Studies in Women's Literature 15.

Nietzsche, F. (1882) The Portable Nietzsche, New York: The Viking Press.

Sartre, J.P. (1938) Nausea, Harmondsworth: Penguin Books.

Icarus Rising

Nigel Pearce

This thing of darkness I acknowledge mine":
Jungian analysis of The Tempest(Prospero and Caliban).

"Tumult and peace, the darkness and light –
Were all the workings of one mind".
- Wordsworth (1805).

This analysis will argue that Shakespeare's 'The Tempest'
functions on many levels: 1) the tempest as an allegory 2) that the
play can be understood, persuasively, by applying a model of
Jungian psychology to it 3) in this context Caliban is a projection of
Prospero's unconscious and, finally 4) that Prospero's achieves
"individualization" by accepting his "darkness".

"(by individualisation I mean) becoming a
single homogenous being...Becoming
one's own self...oming into selfhood".
- Jung (1963).

Firstly, the backdrop to the drama is conflict: a storm rages. The
idea of a tempest is embedded in the Western cultural tradition
which emanates, to an extent, from the Judeo-Christian perspective
of which Shakespeare would have been aware. This is manifest in
the Old Testament where a storm is perceived as the consequence
of repression of natural forces or a birth trauma:

"or who shut up the sea with doors, when
it brake forth, as if it had issued out of the womb".
- The Bible (1601).

However Shakespeare enhances the traditional image to give it an
egalitarian orientation:

"What cares these roarers for the name of King?"
- Shakespeare (1987).

This storm is a symptom of inner conflict within Prospero and is
therefore, in turn, his allegorical reality:

"(The Tempest) is an example of
allegory the leading characters are
not merely typical but symbolic".
- Lowell (1868/1890).

The world of symbols is significant in psychology; Freud believed
that they existed in the "unconscious" and were repressed material
expelled from the "ego" {see Freud (1900)}. However Jung
developed this concept to embrace a "collective unconscious"; a
world of primal images which occur consistently in humanity's
mythology and religions {see Jung (1967)}.These recurring or primal
symbols he called "archetypes." The philosophical dimension of
Jung's psychology can be located in Plato's 'Theory of Forms' {see
Grube (1980)}, here the "Idea" exists in a pure "Form" beyond the
material world in the same way that Jung's symbols exist beyond

consciousness. But Jung expanded his theory of symbols to describe a more precise element of the unconscious:
"a symbol was a particular manifestation
of something unknown".
- McLynn (1996).
One of these "particular" symbols, for this analysis, is the island where the drama is enacted which is a "projection" (Jung) of inner worlds:
..the isle is full of noises

....

Sometimes a thousand twanging instruments
Will hang about my ears ".
- Shakespeare (1987).
The onomatopoeia of "twanging" enforces this sense.

On the island the relationship between Prospero and Caliban was an exploitative one. Prospero treats Caliban as a slave by day and torments him at night. I would like to examine their relationship in the context of contemporary cultural sources. Firstly, Caliban is an anagram of "cannibal", spelt "canibal" in Shakespeare's era, secondly that Shakespeare would have been aware of, in particular, Montaigne's essay: 'Of the Caniballes' in which "primitive" societies are seen as natural until tainted by civilisation:
" Montaigne is saying that the life of the
South American Indians proves that mankind
Is capable of living peacefully, happily and
humanly
without the constraint of law, or the institution of
private property".
- J.Middleton Murry (1936)
This is reflected by Gonzalo's speech on utopia:
"I' the commonwealth
I would admit; no name of magistrate ...
... Riches, poverty service none
No occupation, all men idle "
- Shakespeare (1987).

Hence Caliban can be perceived as a member of a, potentially, utopian community and Prospero as the corrupting force of civilisation. Hence Caliban is perceived as the "primitive" (unconscious) and Prospero as civilisation (conscious).

This idea can be developed by applying Jung's conception of the feminine perspective which he believed to emanate from the 'Great Mother' archetype:

"She has always been connected with the
moon and the earth...she was and is
the matrix from which all is born".
- Von der Heydt (1976).

This analysis maintains that, following Jung, the feminine is the source of creativity {See Graves (1961) for a theory of the feminine as 'Lunar Muse'} .Therefore it is
possible to argue that Caliban is in tune with his, to use Jung's term, Anima (the unconscious feminine) i.e. the creative/primitive (Earth) aspect of his psyche:

"   ..Caliban!
Thou (being of the) Earth speak...
- Shakespeare (1987)

Caliban can therefore be comprehended as the source of the play's creativity. This is stressed, by Shakespeare, as Caliban speaks in poetry and Prospero in prose. Caliban's role as a vehicle for creative energy and of his being, therefore, in tune with nature and poetry is illustrated in the following passage:

...   ...in dreaming,
methought the clouds would open ...
....
Ready to drop on me; when I wak'd,
I cried to dream again.
- ibid.

This passage is beautiful in its poetic innocence.   Coleridge elaborated on this aspect of Caliban's being:

"Caliban...is a sort of creature of the
earth...He is a man in the sense
of imagination."
- Coleridge (1811).

However Prospero's attitude towards Caliban could have been influenced by the attempted rape, by Caliban, of his daughter Miranda.

"In mine own cell till thou dast seek to violate
the honour of my child."
- Shakespeare (1987)

But some Jungian theorists have maintained that this was itself a projection by Prospero of incestuous feelings onto Caliban:

"Incest; the molestation and rape of one's
daughter. Miranda had reached womanhood
with herself and her father as the only two
humans in their world".
- Beck (1993).

Why then is Caliban defined as "other" or "dark". in the play?

The Jungian concept of 'The Shadow' provides an explanation. Jung explains his concept:

> "The shadow personifies everything the subject
> refuses to acknowledge about himself".
> - Jung (1959)."

The ideas that are not accepted become repressed into an unconscious complex: the shadow. There are, essentially, two methods which Jung thought people employ to address their "Shadow": 1) projection i.e. projecting your "shadow"onto another person. or 2) "integration", i.e. the accepting your "shadow" as part of the "Self." Jung thought the latter lead to selfhood and "individualization". Prospero has repressed his "shadow", his moon and Earth dimensions, the Anima which is the source of creativity. The consequences of this were 1) becoming introspective and interested in using manipulation (magic):

> "And to my state grew stranger, being transported
> And rapt in secret studies".
> - Shakespeare (1987).

2) projecting his 'shadow' onto Caliban and using abusive language to describe him:

> "Thou most lying slave...
> Filth thou art...
> - ibid.

This is the generalized "tempest".

Caliban can be seen as a projection of Prospero's "shadow", his unconscious complex which is both creative and destructive.

> "Prospero is afraid of Caliban. He is afraid because
> he knows that his encounter with Caliban is largely
> his encounter with himself".
> - Singh (1996).

Prospero has a choice: either his unconscious will overwhelm him and he will descend into madness or he can integrate his "shadow", Caliban, into himself. Prospero chooses the path of self-integration:

> "This thing of darkness I acknowledge mine".
> - Shakespeare (1987).

He accepts the creative force of the"Anima"and says:

> ...set me free"
> - ibid.

Bibliography

Bible, King James Version (1601).

Beck. B, "Shakespeare's The Tempest:, A Jungian Interpretation, http jung
the tempest.

Coleridge, S.T "Lectures on Shakespeare and Milton" (Macmillian 1991).

Freud. S, The Interpretation of Dreams. ed James Strachey (London 1900).

Graves. R, The White Goddess. (London 1961).

Grube. G, Plato's Thought. (1980).

Jung. C.G, Memories, Dreams, Reflections. (Collins 1963).

Jung. C.G, Man and his Symbols. (Picador 1964).

Jung. C.G The Archetypes and the Collective Unconscious (Routledge 1967).

Lowel.J "Shakespeare once More, Prose Works" vol 3 (1868-1891) in' The
Tempest' York Notes Advanced' ed L.Todd (London 2003).

McLynn.F Carl Jung (Transworld Publishers 1996).

Middleton Murry. J "Shakespeare's Dream" (1936) in "Shakespeare: 'The
Tempest' Casebook Series" ed D.J.Palmer (Palgrave 1991).

Montaigne, M "Of Cannibals" in Donald Frame ed "The Complete Works of
Montaigne".

Shakespeare.W The Tempest, ed Stephen Orgel (Oxford 1987).

Singh. J "Caliban vs Miranda: Race and gender conflicts in Callaghan, Kaplin
and Troube (eds) Feminist re-readings of Early Culture" (C.U .P. 1996).

Von der Heydt. V Prospects for the Soul: Soundings in Jungian Psychology and
Religion (Darton, Longman and Todd 1976)

Wordsworth. W "The Poetical Works of William Wordsworth", Owen and
Smyser eds 3 vols (Clarendon Press 1974). .

Nigel Pearce

The life and ideas of Emma Goldman

Emma Goldman was a woman who defied those who would oppress humanity generally and her specific contribution to the rise of revolutionary feminism is today of major significance. Her refusal to submit to the jackboot of any ideology she regarded as tyrannical, whether it was American capitalism or what she regarded as mistakes made by the Russian Marxists around the Kronstadt uprising in 1921. But revolutionaries never grow old and as a mature woman of 67 she traveled to Spain in 1936 to help organize the defense of the revolution against the fascists and other agents of international Capital. She was both a theoretician and an activist who wrote some of the most important documents of modern anarchism and also spent time in prison because of her refusal to be silenced. Emma was born into a Jewish family living in Lithuania in 1869. But because of the backlash from the state after the assassination of Tsar Alexander 11 in 1881, there was great political oppression and pogroms against Jews, the family moved to St.Petersberg when Emma was 13. As a consequence of their economic hardship she had to leave school after six months and work in a textiles factory. It was here that Emma was introduced to revolutionary ideas and read a novel by Nikolai Chernyshevsky called: What is to be Done in which the heroine Vera becomes a nihilist and lives in a world where there is not any hierarchy in gender relationships and where all work is done on a co-operative basis. Theseexperiences, both emotional and intellectual, would create within Emma a distrust of state authority and a desire for freedom, they created the foundations on which her anarchist politics and philosophy would later be constructed. In 1931 she encapsulated her beliefs succinctly: "I want freedom, the right to self-expression, everyone's right to beautiful, radiant things". - Emma Goldman. By the age of 15 Emma was becoming a lively young woman, her father's response was to get her married, she refused and consequently her parents decided to send her to America. Emma soon realized that the U.S.A. was not the land of opportunity for the masses, but a capitalist system based on exploitation. She married a fellow factory worker and gained U.S. citizenship. Would her life be worn down into dust by capitalist oppression and patriarchy domination? At the age of 20 things were rather bleak, but in 1886 something occurred which would again ignite the fire within Emma. The anarchist movement in the U.S. was quite active at this time and during a clash between militant workers and the police in Chicago, the workers were demanding an eight-hour day, someone threw a bomb into a group of police. Eight anarchists were convicted on very flimsy evidence; the judge even told them they were on trail "because you are anarchists". Four anarchist comrades were hung and became known in working-class history as the Haymarket Martyrs. On the day of the verdict Emma decided to become a revolutionary. HerHer marriage had not been a success so Emma now divorced her husband, moved to New York and joined the community of anarchist thinkers and activists. Emma was realizing that:

"It requires less mental energy to condemn than

to think". - Emma Goldman.

She was thinking and contemplating action: Having traced Emma Goldman's early years to the point where she embraced revolutionary anarchism I would now like to examine four areas of her thought: 1) Her commitment to the concept of "propaganda by deed" which had been developed by the anarchist thinker and activist Mikhail Bakunin. 2) Emma's analysis of religion and the failure of Christianity. 3) Goldman and the Bolsheviks. 4) Her ideas on the nature of love. Emma was initially attracted to anarchists of the Bakuninite tendency who were, in the U.S., grouped around Johann Most. She embraced many of Mikhail Bakunin's ideas because he had argued that anarchism was the:

"absolute rejection of every authority including that which sacrifices freedom for the convenience of the state."

-Mikhail Bakunin.

The position he was arguing for here would not be considered particularly militant in revolutionary circles and formed a basic tenet of anarchist philosophy. However Bakunin's ideas of how to achieve the raising of the consciousness of the oppressed from that of their day to day struggles to that of revolutionary action were radical and are still contested by some anarchists and most Marxists in the anti-capitalist movement today, he argued that:

"we must spread our principles, not with words but with deeds, for this is the most popular, the most potent, and the most irresistible form of propaganda."

- Mikhail Bakunin.

This theory was called "propaganda by deed", it was assumed that a revolutionary act, often of individual violence, would arouse the masses to take place in an insurrection and overthrow the existing order. This was an essential component of Bakunin's political philosophy. He followed this argument to its logical conclusion and perceived the revolutionary's emotions of hostility towards the system as a manifestation of creativity:

"The passion for destruction is a creative passion".

- Mikhail Bakunin.

The reason Bakunin's position is criticized by most Marxist revolutionaries is because it detaches an individual activist from the collective nature of working class struggle. These comrades argue

Nigel Pearce

that revolutionaries should organize themselves in a revolutionary party within the most advanced sections of the working class and when historical necessity creates the circumstances this "vanguard" should intervene in a decisive way. This party of organized activists will, it is argued, play a leading role in guiding the proletariat towards its "world historic task" (Engels) of creating the "dictatorship of the proletariat", which is the rule of the majority. Once created a "workers state" will, as objective conditions allow, "wither away" (Engels) to leave a classless society. Both anarchists and Marxists believe that the creation of a society without class or gender hierarchies is the desirable conclusion of social transformation. Nevertheless Emma was, at this time, convinced of the truth of Bakunin's theory of "propaganda by deed". While in New York she met Alexander Berkman, a friend of Johann Most and follower of Bakunin, Emma and Alexander became lovers and would remain life-long friends. This core of three intellectuals was committed to the idea of "propaganda by deed". Goldman and Berkman closely followed a violent strike taking place in 1912 known as the 'Homestead Strike'. The workers had occupied the factory but were expelled by gunmenhired by the owners, several workers died in the struggle. Emma and Alexander were enraged; Goldman gives an account of their feelings (Frick was the manager):

> "We were stunned. We saw at once that the time for our manifesto had passed. Words had lost their meaning in the face of innocent blood spilled. Intuitively each felt what was surging in the heart of the other. Sasha [Alexander Berkman] broke the silence. "Frick is the responsible factor in this crime," he said; "he must be made to stand the consequences."
>
> It was the psychological moment for an Attentat (i.e., assassination); the whole country was aroused, everybody was considering Frick the perpetrator of a coldblooded murder. A blow aimed at Frick would re-echo in the poorest hovel, would call the attention of the whole world to the real cause behind the Homestead struggle. It would also strike terror in the enemy's ranks and make them realize that the proletariat of America had its avengers".
>
> -Emma Goldman.

Emma then tried, unsuccessfully, to prostitute herself to raise money to buy a gun, but eventually Berkman carried out an unsuccessful assignation attempt for which he was sent to prison for 22 years, being released on parole after 14 years. Berkman had refused to implicate Emma in the action and she campaigned for his release. Johann Most, who had been at the heart of the Bakuninite movement in the U.S., suddenly changed his position, condemned Berkman in his newspaper and accused him of creating sympathy for Flick. Emma continued with her political activities, but was disillusioned with the Bakuninite tactic of "propaganda by deed". She remained an active agitator and shared platforms with the I.W.W. (International Workers of the World) that were an anarcho-syndicalist organization committed to working class struggle. In 1916 Emma was arrested for her feminist activities, she was distributing radical literature to women workers We can see how Emma's Bakuninitestances lead her to make errors in the tactics to be employed by revolutionaries. But her refusal to be gagged by the State, patriarchy or capitalist oppression is something which can be admired today. Next I would like to examine Emma Goldman's ideas about Atheism and Christianity. Her ideas were fine tuned 1913-16. She was to a considerable degree influenced by Fredrick Nietzsche who she describedas a "great mind". His proclamation that "God was dead" resounded through the world of all thinking people in the modern period. For Nietzsche the problem was once there is not a Divine "first cause" or Creator God for Nature then everything is in chaos. How can human beings live authentically in these circumstances? A part of his answer was derived from his reading of Schopenhauer and the concepts of "appearance" and "reality". Nietzsche applied these concepts to Greek culture: the Apollonian seen as the intellectualizing, the world of "appearances", and the Dionysian as the wild and stormy dimension which is tuned into real life or "reality", the "will-to-life", the creative. It was this "will-to life" that Nietzsche and Goldman believed was being suppressed by Christianity and religion in general. Emma said:

> "The Atheists know that life is not fixed, but
> fluctuating, even as life itself is".
> - Emma Goldman.

This is her recognition of the life-force, the Dionysian as opposed to Apollonian. That is not to suggest that Goldman was not an intellectual, for she most certainly was, but that she was in touch with the essence of life itself. An illustration of this occurred on an occasion when Emma was dancing and a young comrade took her to one side and said that this was not correct behavior for an agitator, Emma replied:

> "Our cause should not expect me to behave like a
> nun, the movement should not be turned into a
> cloister, if it means that, I do not want it".
> Emma Goldman.

Of Nietzsche she said:

> "Nietzsche was not a social theorist, but a poet, a rebel
> and innovator. His aristocracy was neither of birth or
> purse; it was of the spirit. In this respect Nietzsche was
> an aarchist"
> Emma Goldman

Her views on political violence underwent a further transformation whilst she was in revolutionary Russia in the early 1920s. Goldman had advocated "propaganda by deed", but had renounced it after the debacle of 1912. However after that period Emma was still in favour of "defensive" working class violence. In revolutionary Russia, she came to the conclusion that the Bolsheviks had institutionalized political violence and terrorism. Her analysis was:

"Such terrorism begets counter-revolution and in   turn becomes counter-revolutionary".

- Emma Goldman.

However she wrote to Berkman in 1926 that there was only one choice open to people: either to become a Bolshevik or a Tolstoy an (Tolstoy had theorized the "Holy Peasant" as the basic unit of the agrarian anarchy-pacifist commune). Tolstoy had said:

"There is only one permanent revolution and that is a moral one: the regeneration of the inner man"

- Leo Tolstoy.

Emma was once asked about her ideas on "free love", she replied:

"Free love? As if love is anything but free! Love is free; it can dwell in no other atmosphere".

- Emma Goldman.

She went on to define her "free love":

"My love is sex, but it is devotion, care, patience, friendship, it is all."

- Emma Goldman.

Icarus Rising

Nigel Pearce

On Turgenev: Fathers and Sons and the nature of Realism in literature

This analysis argues that although literary 'form' is determined by the socio-economic conditions i.e. form is determined by the content it embodies and as the social 'mode of production' changes the nature of that 'content' is transformed and therefore effects the 'form'(see Eagleton (1976). That there is not a 'reflex' connection between them and that by examining the way 'form' is used in Fathers and Sons' (1863), in the light of the modern Realist novel developed by Lukcas. We can comprehend how Realist and non-Realist techniques achieve a 'totality'. I shall argue that Marx (1859) constructs a persuasive theoretical model which can be applied to the Realist Novel. However this must be understood in the context of a 'dialectical' relationship between 'form' and 'content' Hegel (1831). Having applied Lukcas' model to Turgenev (1863) especially his ideas of 'typicality' (by this he means an individualized character combined with a 'world historic' epoch, 'world historic' can defined as a 'progressive' historical epoch e.g. the period in Russia during 1860's) and I argue that because Bazarov was both a 'typical' and 'world historic' character and therefore the novel achieves a 'totality' i.e. a 'balance of 'general and particular and also the conceptual and sensuous' (Eagleton 1976). Was he prime 'New Man in the Realist Novel? I contest this with reference to Turgenev Hamlet and Quixotic (1860). Consequently we can comprehend the roots of thedecline of the Realist Novel into both Naturalism and into Formalism with the concomitant rise of 'irrationalism' Lukcas(1938).I argue that this degeneration originated from the 'idea' of 'the superfluous man' Turgenev (1850) in Russian literature which itself was the product of material conditions. I will illustrate these claims by close reference to the text and in particular contrasting Realist and non-Realist literary techniques. Clear socio-economic forces influenced the 19th century Realist novel a) the convolutions caused in Western Europe would spread West b) the defeat of Imperial Russia in the Crimean War (1853-6) and the rise of the razanochinets new class of educated young men and women who were not aligned with the ruling class and estranged from the 'traditions' and who acted on their beliefs. this concept found its highest manifestation in 'What is to be Done? Cherngyshevsky: (1863). Fathers and Sons is composed of both Realist and non-Realist elements. It's not a political trait that is masquerading as a Realist model and confined by the dictates 'socialist Realism as in 'Mother: Gorky (1903) nor is it an example of 'genre' of another form of distorted Realist form such as 'the Naturalism of Zola in 'Germinal':

By naturalism Lukcas means the distortion of realism
which merely photographs the surface phenomena of
society without penetrating to their significant essences.
(Eagleton (1976) p 28.)

Turgenev employs some basic Realist methods, at the beginning of
the book we are introduced to an 'Omniscient Narrator who can
describe the 'plot' but also, significantly see into the 'essences', the
'totalities' that Lukcas maintains is the central aspect of Realism; If a
writer strives to represent reality as it truly is, i.e. if he is an authentic
realist, then the question of totality plays ad decisive role. ibid.
Turgenev immediately acquaints us with an omniscient narrator i.e.
who both describes and sees beyond the surface:

'We will acquaint the reader with him '
His name is Nicolai Petrovich Korsakov.
(Turgenev (1863) p 1.)

This is immediately 'counter-balanced' by an account of the
Korsakov's own account of his life as both social history in which we
are given unique access to his character not as the product dialogue
but all-seeing narrator; portentously we are told:

but then along came 1848'
ibid p. 5.

The year which revolutions swept Europe. Soon this era is a
connecting passage of 'dialogue' which also has the quality
of'showing:

"Dad let me introduce my good friend Bazarov....'
'Sincerely glad, 'h began, and grateful to you for kindly
intending to stay with us...Permit me to ask your name...'
'Evegeny Vasilev' Bazarov answered in a lazy but manly
voice.
' ibid p.7.

This is an example of both Turgenev's ability to combine Realist
technique and aspects of his 'style' in this dialogue, it is an
apparently straightforward piece of Realism but an 'atmosphere' is
being created:

'As a conjurer of atmosphere Turgenev had no equal.'
(Freeborn (2001). p. 105.)

I would argue that 'atmosphere is similar to 'essence'; Turgenev has
looked beyond the objective 'material reality' in a fashion 'typical' of
Realist technique, indeed here is employing a technique used by
Austin of 'polarized characters' e.g. Elizabeth and Mrs Bennett.
However I would suggest that Turgenev's characters to do possess
that opposition of and 'roundness' and 'flatness respectively found in
the Austin's two mentioned. They are character in a seminal
example of the Realist genre in Pride and Prejudice Austin (1818).
But in the 19th century Realist novel, the characters and in particular

Bazarov transcend this. They develop in the context of their societal circumstances i.e. in the 'content' but the unique 'form' then rebounds to transform the 'content' which, in turn affects the socio-economic conditions from which it has arisen. While juxtaposing Austin and Turgenev it is of interest to examine Freeborn a comment made by Freeborn regarding Turgenev:

> 'he succeeded in creating the world of the ... country estate so perfectly that no other writer has surpassed him.'
>
> - ibid

This is significant in several ways, firstly Freeborn is suggesting the great technical skill in 'showing' and 'telling' to produce the 'totality' of the country estate and secondly the importance of this 'setting' in Turgenev (1863) because of the physical limitations he imposed the characters are is using the technique of 'concentration' in which he characters emotions are intensified and they experience a number of realizations. An example of this is Chapter 17; Odintosva is talking about her life with Bazarov in her 'country estate'. was firstly provided with an example 'telling' by the narrator, this is a fundamental Realist Technique: 'The estate where Anna Sergeevna lived stood on a bare sloping hill a short distance from a yellow stone church with a green roof and white pillars' Turgenev (1883) p 81. I shall attempt to illustrate firstly the complex relationship between 'content' and 'form".The work of the German left-wing Hegelian whose Essence of Christianity (1841) had a major impact in Russia in the 1840's embraced a materialist outlook.' Oxfford (2009) p129 Hence the 'social context of Turgenev (1883) influence its 'content' which acted the 'form' and its automatious development: '

> Art possess a high degree of autonomy.'
>
> -Trotsky (1924)

Baranov's crude Materialism emanates from Feuerbach (1841): He addresses Odintosva:

> 'You're healthy, independent and wealthy-what more could you want?
>
> 'What do I want...yes, I'm old...and ahead of me a long, long road with nothing to aim for...I just don't want to go down it.' 'You're disillusioned.'
>
> -Turgenev (1883) p. 97/8.

Two main aspects of Turgenev's technique are illustrated here 1) the use of dialogue as a means to create characterization but 2) this is an epiphany for both characters a) Baranov begins to see the constraints of pre- Marxist Materialism, b) Odintosva experiences an 'existential crisis' and they both realize they share an estrangement from Russian society and, indeed, the natural world. We can understand how on page 81+97/8 Turgenev uses the 'conjuncture' of 'telling' followed by 'dialogue' to create this moment of realization .

The main emphasis of 'focalization' in Fathers and Sons is on Baranov because he is 'the centre of consciousnesses of the narrative. Bazarov is an example of Turgenev's complex characterization a): he a fictional figure and b) a figure based on a young doctor Turgenev had met and c) a 'typical' character. In 'Studies in European Realism (1972) and The Historical Novel (1962) Lukcas explained his ideas on the Realist novel. As I have illustrated Bazarov embodied what Lukcas called 'typical' character which must live in a 'World Historic' epoch' without being submerged in them and is therefore 'individualized. I would argue that the 1860's as such a period. For Lukcas what created a great realist novelist was not individual ability but:

> the richness and profundity of created characters relies upon the richness and profundity of the social process.

> - New Hungarian Quarterly (Autumn 1972).

Finally, Turgenev although a great Realist writer derived much from non-realist sources and applied then in his novels. In Hamlet and Don Quitiote (1860) they are seen as opposite poles; one introspective, the other lives outside of his psyche and is capable of self-sacrifice This is an non-realist model constructed above, and shows Turgenev' s flaw, his 'superfluous man' (1850) who has radical words but no action can be seen in Bazarov while the prototype for the Bolsheviks would be Chernyshevsky (1863) heroine Vera Pavlovna. Turgenev was not:

> On the threshold of the future Turgenev:

> (Oxford 2001) p 132.

We can comprehend the roots of the decline of the Realist Novel into both Naturalism Lukcas (1938) an originating in the non-Realist' of 'the. We can comprehend the roots of the decline of the Realist Novel into both Naturalism Lukcas (1938) as originating in the non-Realist' of 'the superfluous man' Turgenev (1850).

Nigel Pearce

Bibliography.

Austin, J Pride and Prejudice (1813) Oxford World Classics.

Cherngyshevsky (1863) in ed Cornwael I Routledge Guide to Russian Literature

Routledge. Eagleton, T (1989) Marxism and Literary Criticism Routledge.

Freeborn The Classic Russian Novel in Cornwell, I ed The Routledge guide to Russian Literature. Routledge.

Hegel, F. (1831) Philosophy of Fine Art in Eagleton (1989) Marxism and literary Criticism Routledge.

Lukcas. (1971) The Theory of the Novel London in Eagleton, T (1989) Marxism and literary Criticism Routledge.

Marx, K, (1977) Selected Works OUP. New Hungarian Quarterly, Autumn 1972.
Oxford Nineteenth Century Thought and Literature in Cornwell, I ed The Routledge Guide to Russian Literature Routledge.

Trotsky, L (1924) Literature and Revolution Red Words.

Turgenev (1850) The Diary of a Superfluous Man in Cornwell, N (2001) ed The Routledge guide to Russian Literature Routledge

Turgenev, I Fathers and Sons, Oxford: World Classics

Icarus Rising

Nigel Pearce

Katherine Mansfield
She maintained that her short stories were:

> a cry against corruption. Not a protest – but a cry and
> I mean corruption in the widest sense of the word of
> course.'
>   -Mansfield (1984-96), vol 2 p.54.

Elizabeth Bowen was an Anglo-Irish writer influenced by
Aestheticism with a collection of short-stories published in 1923,
commented on Mansfield:

> The denial of love, the stunting of sorrow, or the
> cheating of joy was to her not short of an enormity.
>   - Bowen (1957), pp. 23-4.

However an analysis founded on psychological biography though of
interest does not place Mansfield in the social and material base of
Modernism . The 'status quo' that is challenged in this reading of
Bliss and At the Bay is patriarchy . This is perceived, in my reading
of Bliss and At the Bay, both in the manifestation of the relationships
as a form of male oppression with the placing of the woman as 'the
Other' in the 'gaze' of the male subject which I suggest Mansfield
subverted. Also following de Beauvoir I agree with her that:

> One is not born, rather one becomes a woman.
>   - de Beauvoir ([1947]1997) Bk 2, p.4

Therefore I reject biological determinism as an explanation for
women's oppression and apply Kaplan (1991)   to illustrate how
Mansfield undermines oppressive male discourses and this to the
centrality of the Modernist literary project. I shall also argue that the
aesthetic techniques Mansfield utilised to articulate these characters
and their effects in the stories challenged patriarchy in its use of
innovatory literary devices. This is seen to manifest itself in the use
of free indirect discourse, narrative disjunction, the plotless story, her
pioneering use of 'one blazing moment' which is what Joyce would
call 'an epiphany' and Woolf 'moments of being' and a poetic
symbolism in her prose. These elements combine to create what
Mansfield said of her writing was 'a kind of special prose.'
(Mansfield, 1997, vol 2, p.33). Therefore I will conclude that in her
writing the manner in which she challenged the status quo is neither
quintessentially aestheticist   or instrumentalist, but is shrouded in
'the mists' which pervade her stories. For as she said:

> I tried to lift the mists from my people and let
> them be seen and then to hide them.
>   - Mansfield, 1984-96, vol. 1, pp. 330-1

This is described as 'Mansfield's innovatory marriage of symbolism
and realism.'   (Della Da Sousa Correa, 2005) p. 76 . She

was indeed a significant Modernist writer who deftly burrowed away at the prevailing status quo. However I will agree with Leon Trotsky that:

> Art, it is said, is not a mirror, but a hammer: it does not reflect, it shapes.
>
> - Trotsky (1924) Ch. 4, p.120.

In Bliss (1918) Mansfield adopts the woman's narrative 'point of view' to challenge patriarchy. Here with 'free independent discourse' (Della Da Sousa Correa, 2005) p. 93 or specifically here 'first person internalized thought' in a 'first person narrator'. As any narrator of this sort is potentially an 'unreliable narrator' because of the 'lack of narrative distance', this in itself erodes the status quo:

So Bertha Young:

> What do you do when you are thirty and turning the corner of the street, you are overcome, suddenly, by a feeling of bliss – absolute - bliss.
>
> -Mansfield (2002) p 174.

The use of ellipse here suggests that there are gaps in her apparent ecstatic state. The narrative is disrupted in its first sentences allowing for narrative space which allows a looser and diverse reading. This apparently irrational 'bliss' is an 'internalized' and 'reflected' 'double'. Dostoevsky 'The Double' (1846) introduced the idea of the 'double', here it is complexified and as Pamela Dunbar notes is 'lesbian desire.'

> Bliss (1918) engages in an expansive way-though still indirectly – with lesbian desire.
>
> - Dunbar (1997) p 104.

Followed by

> How idiotic civilisation is! Why be given a body if you have to keep it shut up in a case like a rare, rare fiddle.
>
> - Mansfield p.174.

Here we may read this as a critique of the masculine world, but as Kaplan in Katherine Mansfield and the Origins of Modernist Fiction points out:

> It is important to restate here Mansfield's refusal to establish difference as the centre of her poetics...As with her distaste for Lawrence's obsessive characterizing of all things as either male or female.
>
> - Kaplan (1992) p. 166.

So I would argue that Mansfield's short-stories are more complex than a female Lawrence, she is more ingenuous than that. Bertha's interior voices do exclude her husband who she has never 'felt

Nigel Pearce

desire' for until that evening. But the exterior narrative does not so obviously with a heterosexual conclusion . However she does feel a lesbian desire for Pearl Fulton in her 'the secret world':

> As she did always fall in love with beautiful women who had something strange about them.
> - Mansfield (2002) p.177.

Mansfield then uses the poetic symbolism of the lunar muse, a special place for women, both mysterious and dark with the depths of a musing with the full moon as alluded to in Prelude Mansfield (2002) p114:

> Bright moonlight hung upon the lifted oars [of the Aloe]... Do you feel it too' said Linda to her mother' as though they spoke in their sleep from some hollow cave.

This is the primordial language of women as described in Robert Graves (1984) The White Goddess. And here again in Bliss

> I do believe this happens between women. Never men', thought Bertha.
> - Mansfield (2002) p. 182

> And the two women stood side by side looking at the tender flowering tree'... - almost to touch the rim of the round silver moon.
> - ibid p. 183.

We can see the synthesising of poetic devices such as simile and metaphor in the prose structure here . But Bertha Young's love for Pearl Fulton becomes a painfully ironic female love when she sees Pearl in her husband's arms. Here we have lesbian love 'in the secret self' challenging patriarchy on a symbolic level almost beyond the comprehension of men as Kaplan (1991) pp.114-117 suggests like the 'female orgasm'. Here we have an unfulfilled 'one blazing moment', a Joycean epiphany that is not a revelation in the World . An alternative perspective on 'the tree' could be the 'Tree of Knowledge' in Genesis Bk 1 where Eve plucks the apple to precipitate the Fall, but that requires a Patriarchal viewpoint which Mansfield does not offer the reader here, indeed the patriarchs are excluded from the garden by the women's 'special sign' (ibid, p 182). This is an example of the synthesis of realism and symbolism which Mansfield called 'a special type of prose' Mansfield, 1997, vol 2, p.33 and which is notable in modernist writing. What is particular to Mansfield, I would maintain, is her blurring the boundaries between poetic and prose styles. This is more radical than just synthesizing Realism and Symbolism and as it undermines any sense of an absolute genre, this undermines the literary 'status quo.' The site of 'gender' as the 'self' as 'subject' is never solidified as a narrator, and it is therefore contested and reflects the manner in which her literature articulates the 'lived experience' of woman in the modern epoch. So we have multiple voices here, it is dialogic in method. Mansfield in the genre of her choice, the story -story, a Modernist form in itself, uses these techniques in creating a transient sense of characterization. Her literary style is both innovatory and complex and places it at the heart of literary Modernism.

Beryl and Mrs Kember in the At the Bay do 'deliberately challenge the status quo' with a more fully developed lesbian reading (see Kaplan (1992, p. 218).The reader can also understand a sort of inner matriarchy when Stanley leaves for work and the woman celebrate and bond.

> Yes, she was thankful. Into the living room she ran, and called. 'He's gone. Linda cried from her room: Beryl! Has Stanley gone? Old Mrs Fairfield appeared, carrying the boy in his little flannel coatee.
> 'Gone?'
> 'Gone!
> Oh the relief, the difference it made to have the man out of the house'.
> - Mansfield (2002) p. 287.

The celebrations and female bonding transcend social class as Alice the 'servant-girl' who with the zest of the Parisian revolutionary masses guillotining the aristocracy:

> Oh, these men!' said she, and she plunged the teapot into the bowl and held it under the water even after it had stopped bubbling, as if it too was a man and drowning was too good for them.
> - ibid p. 288.

It is a veritable 'festival of the oppressed' (Marx) celebrating the removal of a hated if idiotic tyrant personified as Stanley . She uses a combination of literary devices in this short passage. It is indeed employing a combination of semi omniscient third-person narrator using multiple voices, dialogue and domestic symbolism with a resonance with the 'ducking stools' used in Shakespeare's England for unruly or outsider women. Mansfield has brewed up a veritable celebration of The Goddess, a witches Sabbath in a domestic caldron. It is focalized by multiple characters.

Section VI illustrates the refusal of Linda Burnell to confirm to biologically pre- determined roles for women as she says to her baby while he smiles at her:

> I don't like babies.
> - Mansfield (2002) p 296.

Here At the Bay foreshadows the theoretical contributions of Simone de Beauvoir. Mansfield provides us with what Kaplan calls 'the anti-archetypal male' in Jonathon Trout. He is an example of the man in which the process of socialization in a patriarchal society has not fully succeeded in producing an oppressive automated male. He is a dreamer disliking the protestant work-ethic in which Stanley comically glorifies. We can see how in At the Bay which reworks Prelude and continues Mansfield's portrayal of the Burnell family. But as Dunbar (1997 p.157) notes she is concerned now with universal rather than psychological themes. When Jonathan Trout is talking to Brenda:

> And all the while I'm thinking, like that moth, or the butterfly or whatever it is. "The shortness of life! The shortness of life!" I've one day or one night, and there's this vast dangerous garden, waiting out there, undiscovered, unexplored,
>
> - ibid p 308

The twelve sections of At the Bay are reflecting the twelve hours of the day. However it is an eternity caught in a day. The influence of Nietzsche's 'Death of God, Darwin's evolutionism and the triumph of scientific Physicalism is apparent here on literary Modernism. So we have' Pater (1873) who influenced Mansfield and Modernism:

> Not the fruit of experience but experience itself - the continual vanishing away, the strange perpetual weaving and unweaving of ourselves.'
>
> - Pater [1873] (2005) p.36

In conclusion Katherine Mansfield was indeed a significant Modernist writer who burrowed away at the prevailing status quo. However I agree with Kaplan (1991) that:

> It is a Modernism full of doubts, questionings, and terrors, but it is a Modernism that leaps beyond the despair of the 'wasteland' and the hierarchical, traditional escapes from it provided by many of her male contemporaries.
>
> - Kaplan (1991) p. 219.

Thus I maintain that Mansfield has asked some important questions which do indeed undermine the foundations of a society which she knew was riddled by 'corruption' (Mansfield (1984-96), Vol 2 p.5), but she offers only provisional solutions. I think the Russian woman writer Alexandra Kollontai in Love of Worker Bees ([1923]1982) presents a character Vasya who as belonging to a social movement, Russian Revolution, challenged both patriarchy and capitalism. Kollontai also suggested a solution to the problems of patriarchal capitalism:

> In place of the individual and egotistic family, there will rise a great universal family of workers, in which all the workers, menand women, will be above all, workers, comrades.
>
> - Kollontai ([1920]1998) p.48.

This leaves the dilemma of the modernist writer. Should he or she enter into a dialectical relationship with the questions they pose, should they provide the answer? I would maintain that Katherine Mansfield perhaps erred on the aesthetic, the posing of questions and this reflected her objective class position as a member of the bourgeois avant-garde.

Nigel Pearce

Bibliography

Bowen, E. (1957) 'Introduction', K. Mansfield, 34 Short Stories, Oxford, Clarendon Press: Collins

de Beauvoir, S. ([1947] 1997) The Second Sex, London: Vintage Classics.

da Sousa Correa, D (2005) The stories of Katherine Mansfield Aestheticism & Modernism: debating Twentieth- Century Literature 1900-1960., Milton Keynes, Routledge, Open University Press.

Dunbar, P. (1997) Radical Mansfield: Double Discourse in Katherine Mansfield's Short Stories, London, Macmillan Press Ltd

Graves, R. (1984) The White Goddess, London: Faber and Faber.

Kaplan, S.J. (1991 Katherine Mansfield and the Origins of Modernist Fiction, London: Cornell University Press.

Kollontai, A. ([1920] 1998) Alexandra Kollontai on Women's Liberation, London: Bookmarks.

Kollontai, A. ([1923] 1983) Love of Worker Bees, London: Virago.

Mansfield, K (1984-96) The Collected Letters of Katherine Mansfield, ed. by V.O' Sullivan and M. Scott, 4 vols, Oxford: Clarendon Press.

Mansfield, K (1997) The Katherine Mansfield Notebooks, ed. by M. Scott, 2 vols, Canterbury, NZ: Lincoln University Press; Wellington, NZ: Daphne,Brasell Associates.

Mansfield, K (2002) Selected Stories, ed. and intro. by A. Smith, Oxford World Classics, Oxford: Oxford University Press.

Pater, W (1873) 'Conclusions', Studies in the History of the Renaissance, London: Macmillan.

Trotsky, L, ([1924] 1985) Literature and Revolution, Chicago: Haymarket Books.

Icarus Rising

Nigel Pearce

Preliminary Notes on philosophy

1) 'Is personal identity a matter of bodily continuity?'

The question of personal identity is of concern to us because we are thinking self-conscious beings. There are two major divisions within philosophy generally; Physicalism and Idealism. The former are concerned with explanations which include matter rather than spirit, a material base for consciousness. The latter are inclined rather to see consciousness as independent of physical being. The debate around personal identity was begun by John Locke, he was replying in some ways to the 'received authority' of Aristotle and the doctrines of the church. However his analysis as the first of the British Empiricists was innovatory. He saw human beings as not being born with *a priori* knowledge but rather being *tabular rosa* i.e. a black sheet upon which impressions are made. Therefore, we are in a new situation with Locke in that the human identity is something we create.

For Locke there was the question of the culpability of the individual, before the Law and eschatologically. He therefore tried to establish the true nature of human identity in this context. For him, it was a 'forensic' question. He differentiated between the bodily continuity and the psychological. Calling the physical human a 'man' i.e. a physical living being who ages over time. But for Locke it was essential to establish the essential nature of human identity. For this he used the term 'person'. A person' was

'a rational thinking thing conscious of itself for itself'
                                                        - John Locke.

Therefore it was 'psychological rather than bodily continuity that Locke was concerned with. He used the 'thought-experiment' of 'The Prince and The Cobbler' to illustrate this as follows: The Prince wakes up in the body of the Cobbler, and the Cobbler wakes up in the body of the Prince. because for Locke personal identity is established by 'psychological identity over time' the identity of the Prince now is truly in the body of the Cobbler, but for Locke culpability is to do with psychological identity rather than bodily continuity.

This created a new 'conversation' about the nature of physical identity. Locke was answered by Thomas Reid who thought his position could not be held logically. Reid used the 'thought experiment' of the young boy and the Calvary officer as follows: a young boy steals an apple from tree, then as a young man is distinguished in battle, but as a mature General cannot remember the act of the child. Now for Locke he would not have been culpable but /Reid saying this is illogical because it denies the 'transitive relation' of: A=B, B=C and therefore A=C. thus for Reid there is continuity of psychological memory with a material base i.e. the 'Calvary officer'

David Hume would answer them both saying that true to Empiricism we should stay rooted a *posterori* experience. So he looked d to his experiences and 'introspected' and found that there nothing but a series of actors crossing the stage of life. We seem to be different people at different times, he called this is called 'the bundle theory of the self', we are fragmented and Hume never resolved the matter of our being a coherent psychological being.

Therefore I would maintain that our psychological community is important and agree with Hume that it is not cohesive over time. I would suggest the following Marx:

> 'Consciousness does not determine being, but rather social being determines consciousness.
>
> - Marx.

2) The argument from design.

The argument from design is made as a rational justification for the existence of a Deity. It is stronger than the argument by faith alone, called fideism. This is because knowledge demands evidence and a theist is on stronger ground if they can employ reasoned arguments rather than a Kierkegaardian 'leap of faith' or 'Pascal' Wager'. The essential concept of argument from design is that there is an argument by analogy from the design in the world and an intelligent designer of the world who is called God.

Therefore in *Dialogues concerning Natural Religion* as the world was in tumult intellectually after the Enlightenment Hume posed the position in the form which Plato employed in his discourses, the 'Socratic discourse' when an philosophical argument is talked through but in order to how the weakness of one.

Cleanthes and Philo dispute the merits off the arguments from design. Firstly Cleanthes argue s that the world resembles one large machine, The argument follows that human beings create structures such as houses and they use intelligence and planning to do so. Therefore it follows by analogy that there must be an intelligent designer of the world who we can call God.

For an argument by analogy to be held two steps are miscarry 1) the uncontroversial case A must be true and there must be an similar 'carry over' to the controversial case B, it must also be true that there is a difference between case A and B or there could not be an analogy to answer,. Thus in an argument from design there must be order in the world which carries over to an intelligent designer who is called God. In the case of Cleanthes and Philo points out two weaknesses, a) there may be a team of builders who constructs the house and for this intelligent design to carry over to a monotheistic

Nigel Pearce

God, there could only be one and b) there is ample dissimilitude to make the analogy weak.

William Paley attempted to answer these weaknesses by using the Watch Makers Analogy

Premise 1. A watch is found on a beach it shows evidence of precise design.

Premise 2. The world also shows evidence of precise order. An eye.

Conclusion There is an intelligent designer of the world and we call (him) God.

But although this position has greater cogency as an analogy because of its 'functionality and precision' it was not held with the development of evolutionary science by Darwin and in particular the method of 'natural selection'. Thus biological organisms were self-selective and self- generating. This to quote Darwkin made the 'watch maker blind'

However does this explain who the creation of life came about in the first place Swinburne argued for a 'fine-tuning argument, i.e. that the cosmological constants needed to create the universe could have come together out of contingency, there had to be 'fine-tuning' and thus a Designer. Against this one could argue that if one bought a ticket in a lottery and won it would be by chance. And maybe the world is not a good outcome as argued Schopenhauer

3) Rawls and Nozick on distributive justice

John Rawls 'A Theory of Justice' (1971) was an attempt to answer the utilitarian position from within the Liberal tradition but with egalitarianism as an inherent aspect.

For Rawls if you were born with a talent you would deserve benefits from the excising of that talent, but his was a significant and revolutionary piece of political philosophy. It deals with the question of 'distributive justice' i.e. who should get what and in what circumstances. In order to develop his innovatory ideas he developed a particular method to answer this problem. How can one start to answer the question of who gets what? Rawls used a unique methodology:

1) The Original Position. This is a thought experiment in which a person does not know their talents, disabilities but has a basic knowledge of economics and politics.

2) The Veil of Ignorance: this is the technique whereby we capacities are hidden.

Rawls thought that if his thought experiment was conducted successfully then two basic principles would be discerned which were differentiated by the 'lexical principle'.

The first of these is the Liberty Principle i.e. everyone has the right to freedom and protection and to allow self-fulfilment or in Aristotle's a term *eudemonia*. He was also influenced by Kantian deontological ethics in that the universiability principle was significant. This leads to his second principle which has two components:
a) Social Equality .and b) 'maximise the minimum' in which the worst off are given the best outcomes in worst situation. Therefore he ordered that we should live in a patterned society in which individual talent is rewarded but the most vulnerable protected. His was a model of meritocratic welfarism.

Answering Rawls Nozick in his *Anarchy, the State and Utopia* (1974) argued that, parodying Marx's

> 'From each according to need to each according to his abilities'.

He argued:

> 'From each according to his chances to each according to each to What they are given.'

his book however was an answer directly to Rawls. He develops a method with a 'thought experiment'. Wilt Chamberlin, an American baseball player, is given 25c for each appearance, he is good at his career and people decide to spend their e money on seeing him. He accumulates $250.00 which is more than others in his society. For Nozick this movement away from a pattern society D1 where people have their money controlled to D2 where people freely spend money on whoever has the best talents or products. In D2 there will not be patterning indeed Nozick argues that paying taxes to 'forced labour'.

A problem with Rawls is that he presupposes certain aspects of Liberalism; individual or at least not 'social' ownership of the means of production and the individual as an agent as opposed to the social.

A problem with Nozick is he almost returns to the State of Nature described by Thomas Hobbes in *'The Leviathan'*

> 'a warre of every man upon all'.

Rather a solution I would argue that Rawls is an advance in that the state exists with the Difference Principle to protect the vulnerable and against Nozick who argues only for 'a night watchman state' where talents are not necessary rewarded but only the strongest and most ruthless succeed.

an analogy between the state/citizen relation and the parent/child relation useful in explaining a citizen's obligation to the state?

An analogy of the state/citizen relation to the parent/child relation is articulated by Plato in a Socratic dialogue in Crito:

> What complaint, pray, do you have against the city and ourselves? That you should now attempt to destroy us? Was it not we who gave you birth
>
> - Plato (1997) p. 73.

The question of whether an analogy between the state/citizen and parent/child explain the citizen's obligations to the state is central to this question. Therefore I will examine the structure of arguments by analogy. I will do this by examining another significant argument by analogy that of William Paley for argument from design. The argument by analogy requires three components. That the first or 'uncontroversial case' must be held, second that there is not a disanalogy between the 'uncontroversial case and the 'controversial case' and third for an argument by analogy there is inherently the necessity for the first or 'uncontroversial case' and the second or 'controversial case' to be differentiated or there would be no possible analogy. Therefore it follows that if in the example of Paley's thought experiment if you were walking on a beach and you find a watch and he makes an analogy between the working of the watch and because they interact in an intelligent or 'functional way' he can attempt to make the case for argue from design between the watch/ world and designer/God. There must be evidence of the functionality of the watch for some form of design to be held to exist, if there was no evidence of function in the watch there can be no analogy with the world, the analogy would fall on the first case. So we can argue the functionality of the watch generates the necessity of a designer. Then the argument follows that we notice evidence of design in the world, there seems to be evidence of complex design in the human eye or in the composition of a leaf of grass. Paley then extrapolates from this first case to an analogous leap to the necessity for there to be a Designer of the human eye of the world of nature, the analogy seems to work. The 'uncontroversial case' is held, there is an analogy between their being a designer of the watch and functionality, we perceive design or function in the world. Therefore there must be a designer who made the watch and thus a Designer who created ordered systems in the world of Nature, an Intelligent Designer who the argument goes is God. Now this works as an argument by analogy because the first case stands and the inference to its conclusion is not dis-analogous and the watch and the world are not the same thing so there is an analogy to be answered. But it is an argument from induction in that we generalize from the evidence to a conclusion. An argument from analogy is not a deductively valid argument. As an example of how an analogy functions William Paley's is a good one, it collapsed though when Darwin proved that species are generated by 'natural selection. I have illustrated my argument in this way in order to show, by way of an example how an argument by analogy is structured.

As I have looked at the mechanics of an argument by analogy is some detail I shall now apply that specifically to the question of the robustness or not of the child/parent analogy is to the citizen/state in Plato's Crito. The figure below illustrates the position:

Figure 1.2   The parent–state analogy

- Pike (2011) p. 20.

The question is one of a benefits argument: a) what benefits does the hypothetical parent provide their child and if they can be carried over to b) the benefits which the state provides for its citizens. Essentially the hypothetical parent will provide a number of things, subsistence, safety and protection; These are the means of subsistence necessary for human existence as Fredrick Engels said at the funeral of Karl Marx:

> Just as Darwin discovered the law of development or organic nature, so Marx discovered the law of development of human history: the simple fact, hitherto concealed by an overgrowth of   ideology, that mankind must first of all eat, drink, have shelter and clothing, before it can pursue politics, science, art, religion, etc.; that therefore the production of the immediate material means, and   consequently the degree of economic development attained by a given people or during a given epoch,   form   the   foundation   upon   which   the   state institutions, the legal conceptions, art, and event the ideas on religion, of the people concerned have been evolved,and in the light of which they must, therefore, be explained, instead of vice versa, as had hitherto been the case.

- Engels, [1883] (1973) p 426

Therefore the benefits the parents give the child are analogous if they are reproduced by the state to the citizen. If this works thinkers like John Rawls believe that the State should 'maximise the minimum' to create the condition in which the citizen may have the opportunity to experience Aristotelian flourishing or eudemonia. Aristotle argued that we are 'political animals' that is we live in the polis which can be defined broadly as a state with a sense of community. He argued further that:

> the state came into being as a means to protect life, it continues in existence in order to secure the good life.
> - Aristotle, in Cottingham (2011) p 622.

In a manner this begs the question as it should (a) parent/state must provide benefits in order for (b) the child/ citizen to prosper for the analogy to pass the first case. If it does not do this there are no benefits then there is no case to answer. It is certainly true in the present economic circumstances the (a) may be struggling rather with the consequence of that which leads to (b) hardship, welfare cuts. Therefore for a benefits argument to work by analogy the benefits must be apparent in the first case and carried over in the second. That is my basic structure. I would argue that it can fail in the first case, because you cannot argue that a hypothetical parent-child relation is consistent enough once you remove the bonds of patriarchal authority. Therefore if this fails Socrates has no obligations to Athens, he may feel he has duties of a Kantian nature but these are not obligations if the analogy has failed. Once patriarchal authority is answered there is no 'benefits argument' between parent and child. It would be the same if Paley's watch wasn't functional; it doesn't 'work' as philosophical analogy. Secondly, the first and second case is dis-analogous because tone is an objective relationship and the other, subjective.

I shall examine a number of philosophical perspectives and a methodology to sketch a context of the citizen's obligation is central to the questions to the state in relation to the question of the structure of 'argument by analogy'. John Rawls (1971) A Theory of Justice attempted to create the theoretical framework for a 'fair-play' argument with his 'Difference Principle':

Alex Callinicos points out that in Rawls (1971) A Theory of Justice:

> The difference principle which involves a deeper form of equality   equality of opportunity, at least as normally understood.
>
> Like many revolutionary works, A Theory of Justice is deeply embedded in the tradition from which it emerged- in this case classical liberalism.and also that in order to understand...A theory is often best understoodby considering what it is written against. In Rawls case this is Unitarianism.
> - Callinicos (2007) p.42.

This tendency was best represented by its founder, Jeremy Bentham

An action then may be said to be comfortable to the principle ...when the tendency it has to augment the happiness of the community is greater than to diminish it.

- Bentham (1982) pp12-13

Philosophical anarchists argue that no political obligations can be successfully held between the citizen and the state. Marxist political philosophers would present a different perspective and a different methodology. A Liberal like John Locke would presume there are obligations on both sides both the citizen and the state. Locke makes the point that a citizen may give 'tacit consent' to the authority of the state:

...whether it be barely travelling feely on the highway...

- Locke, 1690, in Cottingham (2011) p. 640.

Rawls claims to have addressed these questions while Libertarians on the political New Right like David Novack in turn argued against his principle of 'maximize the minimum', the best outcomes in the worst case, by arguing for a state to exist merely as a guardian of property rights.

An analogy of the state/citizen relation to the parent/child relation is articulated in Plato Crito and began a discourse on the nature of the relationship between citizen and the state which is at the core of Western political philosophy. In this way it is something akin to the organic analogies in the human. The two relationships which Plato characterises in Crito, by analogies, are firstly that of the relationship of children to their parents and secondly the relationship of the slave to the master. I shall concentrate on the former but recognize the latter in this dialectic.

Plato uses the case of the aging Socrates condemned to death by the state for denying the state religion and spreading dissident concepts amongst the youth to explore the nature of this argument from analogy. However is there a benefits argument to be had in the parent/child and citizen/state relationship? What rights and obligations are involved? So is any relationship of an implicit nature as Locke argues is not convincing for not many make a conscious and explicit commitment to the state. Do the citizenry rather give up their sovereignty to an Absolute Ruler in return for protection from a life which would otherwise be 'a warre of all on all' which would be 'nasty and brutish and short' Hobbes argued in his important text ,'The Leviathan'. I would argue however it is a process of socio-historical Necessity that defines the citizen's orientation to the state:

. It is not the consciousness of men that determines their being, but, on the contrary, their social being determines their consciousness.

- Marx [1857] (2007) p. 425

Nigel Pearce

My findings are: 1) if patriarchal authority is not accepted then in the first case this analogy fails, 2) the analogy is not robust in-itself i.e. it does not 'carry-over' and 3) if positions #1 and #2 are held even if you accept patriarchal authority then you should bit the bullet and argue for a necessary 'social transformation'. This is required because even if the analogy works as benefits/fair-play argument which is really neo-Liberalism and Rosa Luxemburg has argued eloquently liberalism or the fair-play/benefits argument can be articulated as:

> the hard core of social inequality and lack of freedom
> hidden underthe sweet shell of formal equality and
> freedom.'

- Luxemburg (1970) p.393.

Hence we are left with a dilemma. I have argued that the analogy in question is not robust, Rawls only adapts liberalism and Novack rejects any obligation on the state except 'night-watchman'. A solution to the problem of the failure of the child/parent analogy with citizen/ state would be a workers state acting and controlled by the majority which then 'withers away' (Engels) leaving Communism as the true dawn of human History where there would be a genuine benefits to all, socialized benefits in a socialized state:

'From each according to his abilities too each according to their needs'

- Marx [1875] (2007) p.615.

Icarus Rising

Bibliography

Aristotle (300 BC) Politics in Cottingham, Western Philosophy: an anthology, Oxford, Blackwell Publishing.

Bentham, J (1982) An Introduction to the Principles of morals and Legislation, London.

Callinicos, A (2007) Equality, Cambridge, Polity Press.

Cottingham, J (2011) [ed] Western Philosophy: an anthology, Oxford, Blackwell.

Engels, F [1883] (1973) Marx & Engels Selected Works, London, Lawrence and Wishart.

Locke, J (1690) Second Treatise of Civil Government in Cottingham (2011) [ed] Western Philosophy: an anthology, Oxford, Blackwell Publishers.

Luxemburg, R (1970) Rosa Luxemburg Speaks, New York.

Marx, K [1875] (2007) Critique of the Gotha Programme in Karl Marx Selected Writings, Oxford, Oxford University Press

Marx, K [1875] (2007) Preface to the Critique of Political Economy in Karl Marx Selected Writings, Oxford. Oxford University Press

Pike, J (2011) Exploring Philosophy, Book 6 Political Philosophy, Milton Keynes, The Open University,

Plato (1995) Defence of Socrates, Euthyphro and Crito. Oxford, Oxford World Classics.

Lightning Source UK Ltd.
Milton Keynes UK
UKOW04n1916110315

247706UK00003B/15/P